YOU WON'T
LIKE ME
WHEN I'M
ANGRY.

HULK

THE ILLUSTRATED SCREENPLAY

FOREWORD BY ANG LEE
INTRODUCTION BY JAMES SCHAMUS

Story by James Schamus
Screenplay by
John Turman and Michael France
and James Schamus

Based on the Marvel
Comic Book Character Created by
STAN LEE and JACK KIRBY

A NEWMARKET PICTORIAL MOVIEBOOK

Newmarket Press
New York

This book is published in the United States of America.

First Edition

10 9 8 7 6 5 4 3 2 1
1-55704-585-2 (Paperback)

10 9 8 7 6 5 4 3 2 1
1-55704-597-6 (Hardcover)

Library of Congress Cataloging-in-Publication Data available upon request.

QUANTITY PURCHASES

Companies, professional groups, clubs, and other organizations may qualify for special terms when ordering quantities of this title. For information, write Special Sales Department, Newmarket Press, 18 East 48th Street, New York, NY 10017; call (212) 832-3575 or (800) 669-3903; fax (212) 832-3629; or e-mail mailbox@newmarketpress.com. www.newmarketpress.com

Edited by Linda Sunshine
Designed by Deborah Daly
Photography credits: Peter Sorel, Industrial Light & Magic

MANUFACTURED IN THE
UNITED STATES OF AMERICA.

OTHER NEWMARKET PICTORIAL MOVIEBOOKS INCLUDE:

The Art of X2: The Collector's Edition
The Art of X2: The Making of the Blockbuster Film
Gods and Generals: The Illustrated Story of the Epic Civil War Film
Chicago: From Stage to Screen—The Movie and Illustrated Lyrics
Catch Me If You Can: The Film and the Filmmakers
Frida: Bringing Frida Kahlo's Life and Art to Film
E.T. The Extra-Terrestrial: From Concept to Classic
Windtalkers: The Making of the Film about the Navajo Code Talkers
  of World War II
Ali: The Movie and the Man
Planet of the Apes: Re-imagined by Tim Burton
Moulin Rouge: The Splendid Book That Charts the Journey
  of Baz Luhrmann's Motion Picture
The Art of The Matrix
Gladiator: The Making of the Ridley Scott Epic
Crouching Tiger, Hidden Dragon:
  A Portrait of the Ang Lee Film
Titus: The Illustrated Screenplay, Adapted from
  the Play by William Shakespeare
The Age of Innocence: A Portrait of the Film Based on
  the Novel by Edith Wharton
Cradle Will Rock: The Movie and the Moment
The Sense and Sensibility Screenplay and Diaries
Saving Private Ryan: The Men, the Mission, the Movie
Amistad: A Celebration of the Film by Steven Spielberg
Bram Stoker's Dracula: The Film and the Legend

TABLE OF CONTENTS

WALKING A CONSTANT TIGHTROPE
by Ang Lee

The shooting script for *The Hulk* that you have in your hands (it is not so much a screenplay as a reflection in bare words of what we ended up with on screen) gives a good idea of where our journey ended, but is only a shadow of the adventures we had along the way. When I first thought about making this movie I had just finished *Crouching Tiger, Hidden Dragon,* and I called the Hulk my new "Green Destiny"—the name of the famous sword in *Crouching Tiger* that everyone chases and no one seems able to hold on to. The essence of this destiny is its elusiveness, it is a destiny that is never completely fulfilled. And that is what I loved so much about early *Hulk* comic books. The energy of Jack Kirby's drawings and the freedom of the stories Stan Lee created enabled me to dream of even greater flights of fancy and bursts of energy. They dealt with huge issues and fears, and found within those fears the will and imagination to under-

Ang Lee on the Universal back lot during the filming of The Hulk.

stand them. I feel that everyone has a Hulk inside and each of our Hulks is both scary and, potentially, pleasurable. In fact, it's the pleasure that's the scariest thing about them.

I love tackling these huge topics that popular genres are so fearless in presenting to us. I have learned, as with *Crouching Tiger*, not to be fooled by their "pop" surface—they are much more difficult to make work than filmmakers often assume. But that is what is exhilarating about them. And the Hulk tackles two great genres—he is the first Marvel creature who is both monster and superhero. I think it's possible to treat this mixture in a very emotional way. *The Hulk*, like *Crouching Tiger*, is a weird combination of pop culture and realistic drama. I think by nature, these two aspects don't want to get along but I try to mix them.

How much should be realistic? If it's too realistic, how can you believe in a green giant or that people can fly? How to combine something that is visually exciting, very free, almost like a childhood fantasy, with the reality of psychodrama, comedy, romance? These are contradictory elements, but to me, they represent the dilemma of my own life in filmmaking. The toughest thing for a filmmaker is to keep it balanced. It's like walking a constant tightrope and that's a thrill for me.

GOOD LUCK

On the first day of shooting, Ang Lee joins his cast and crew for a Good Luck Ceremony. Performed at the start of every Ang Lee movie, the tradition is meant to show respect.

INTRODUCTION

EMPATHY FOR THE HULK

by James Schamus

Early cell repair concept by ILM's visual effects art director, Wilson Tang, demonstrates to director Ang Lee how the Hulk's cells are healed and reproduced, thus allowing him to gain mass. Tang's idea was to blend Eastern philosophy with the fictional scientific research that Ang Lee and James Schamus brought to the myth of the Hulk.

Rage. It's the first word of Homer's *Iliad*, whose hero, Achilles, has always stood in the Western tradition as a troubling precursor for many of our great epic protagonists. What to make of this overgrown mama's boy, so often petty, pissed off, sulking, and, when called finally to action, murderous? That he also, at the end of Homer's poem, sits and cries, in mutual mourning, with his enemy King Priam, whose sons he has slaughtered, only adds to our confusions about the nature of his heroism, and of the heroic legacy he has left us. For as every reader of Homer knows, Achilles would soon go on to kill more of Priam's people, all the while knowing he himself was doomed to die in Troy.

The big question Achilles poses is one every Hollywood executive and actor asks more or less daily: What's his motivation? But of course that is an unanswerable question in the vocabulary of Achilles' world. A hero is fated, not motivated, and is all too human because his inhuman greatness is an unchosen gift from the Gods. Achilles' flood of rage is a mark of both human psychology and inhuman destiny: the patterns that give his life enduring meaning are precisely those that strip him of his mortal identity.

I write the above basking in the glow of the good news coming out of Hollywood: This past year, the so-called "copyright businesses" such as movies, music, and TV shows have become America's number one export, overtaking weapons, drugs, and food to claim the top spot. You might ask what this has to do with rage? As a writer and a producer of Ang Lee's *The Hulk*, I have a vested interest in the enduring marketability of epics of anger and destruction and the accompanying heroes who perpetrate the mayhem and try to create meaning out of it. Last year's big numbers were driven by films such as

8

Spider-Man, Lord of the Rings, and *Attack of the Clones*, as this year's will no doubt be by *Matrix Reloaded, X-Men 2,* and, I hope, *The Hulk.* Of course, this has also been the year, in the words of the CIA officer quoted at the end of Bob Woodward's *Bush at War*, that "America will export death and violence to the four corners of the earth in defense of our great nation." But unlike the CIA, who *give* their exported violence away, Hollywood gets the world to *pay* for its exports.

Why do audiences at home and abroad so gladly cough up for these privileges? Certainly spectacles of mayhem have always had their pure entertainment value. But on a deeper and more important level, such spectacles hold little fascination without the heroic figures who are inscribed within them. It is the constant testing, reconfiguring, and evolution of such heroes that make these movies so compelling, and the Hulk provides the opportunity to explore a particularly complex member of the heroic tribe.

As first introduced to the world four decades ago in the groundbreaking Marvel comic book series by Stan Lee and Jack Kirby, the Hulk was immediately remarkable as a different kind of hero—perhaps not even a hero at all. Paired in a Jekyll-and-Hyde dyad with ultra-nerd nuclear scientist Dr. Bruce Banner, the Hulk was at once the accidental, Frankensteinian expression of our highest scientific ambitions and the brute, primal cave-dweller that still exists within us all. Emerging from inside Banner at moments of frustration and rage (we all remember the famous tag line from the Hulk TV show, "You're making me angry—you wouldn't like me when I'm angry"), Hulk was a perfect embodiment of American repression, a curiously asexual rampaging Id, a gigantic "No!" shouted out against the technological new world order.

Interestingly, the Hulk is neither superhero nor supervillain; but he is not, as Nietszche would put it, a super-man beyond good and evil either. He is, rather, *before* them—an innocent being, like the cute fifteen-month-old toddler, who one day, without warning, turns into an apoplectic, screaming, hyperventilating tantrum-throwing mini-Hulk—as awe-inspiring a combination of humanity and inhumanity as a person can witness.

Whether he is called a hero or not, Hulk's destructive innocence clears a path that gives us access to the domain of the heroic. The genius of Lee and Kirby's childish creation allows us to connect to a time before memory—a time steeped with emotion, purpose, feeling, and awe, the experience of which forms us in incalculable ways. The Hulk's greatness is the greatness of our children, and, of course, of our *inner* children. And the wonderfully exportable, entertaining fear he inspires is not just the fear of the monster lurking in the shadows, it is the fear of ourselves—a fear which is also the sign of our own connection to the Gods.

THE FIRST SUPERHERO MONSTER

When I was younger, I loved the movie *Frankenstein*, starring Boris Karloff as the monster, and I also loved *Dr. Jekyll and Mr. Hyde*. One day, I figured, "Boy, wouldn't it be cool to combine the two of them and get a character who is a monster who can change from a normal human into the monster?" I always felt that in the movie *Frankenstein*, the monster was really a good guy. He didn't want to hurt anybody, he was just always being chased by those idiots holding torches and running up and down the hills. So I thought, "Why not get a sympathetic monster, but let it be a guy who can change back and forth?" So, the Hulk became the first superhero who was also a monster.

Stan Lee,
creator of the Hulk

THE TV HULK

In 1977, CBS purchased the rights to *The Incredible Hulk* and hired veteran television producer, Kenneth Johnson, a writer for *The Six Million Dollar Man* and the producer of *The Bionic Woman*, to build a hit. His first act as the Hulk's producer: Make some important changes to the story.

Johnson first decided to change Bruce Banner's first name to David in order to depart from the normal alliterative comic book naming formula (Peter Parker, Lana Lang, etc.). Johnson then altered the core story behind Banner's transformation into the Hulk. Instead of Banner being accidentally doused with gamma radiation on a bombsite, he willfully douses himself with radiation in an attempt to test the effects of gamma rays on human strength. Johnson also omitted several of the comic book super villains and government scoundrels and replaced them with more realistic criminals and a relentless, struggling tabloid reporter determined to unmask Banner in order to propel his own career. Finally, while the television Hulk was angry and green like his comic book counterpart, he never spoke and was noticeably more vulnerable than the Stan Lee version.

The two-hour pilot aired in November of 1977 on North American television and surprised both viewers and critics with its dramatic tone, the sophistication of its writing, the intelligence of its star and its poignant moments. The pilot received high ratings and positive reviews from some very surprised critics. The show also earned impressive box-office returns when it was released theatrically in other parts of the world.

Three weeks later, Bill Bixby returned in a second television movie entitled, *The Return of the Incredible Hulk* (also known as *A Death in the Family*). Popular once again, this second two-hour episode introduced audiences to the duality of David Banner—his struggle against the dark, angry creature inside of him. The success of these two episodes gave network executives the confidence they needed in order to launch a full season of *The Incredible Hulk* in the spring of 1978.

The first season of this one-hour drama outperformed expectations and returned for a second season in September of 1978. This second season continued the familiar formula that had won the Hulk popularity with its fans but began to deal more with serious societal issues such as mental illness and alcoholism.

The third season of the series was perhaps the most difficult for its star, Bill Bixby. In an episode entitled "The Psychic" which aired in February of 1980, Bill Bixby costarred with his wife Brenda Benet. Unfortunately, their marriage suffered heavily during this period and the two divorced. Shortly thereafter, Benet took Christopher, her son with Bixby, on a trip to Mammoth Lakes with actor Don Edmonds. Christopher became ill and died suddenly, an event that so shook Benet that she committed suicide in 1982.

As the series approached its fourth season, a series of budget cuts and policy changes became a problem for the series which was ultimately cancelled in the beginning of its fifth season. Production officially stopped in the summer of 1981 and the series went off the air without an official finale in 1982.

When the show ended, Johnson went on to write and direct the popular mini-series *V* and the television series *Alien Nation*, while Lou Ferrigno, who would forever be identified as the Incredible Hulk, went on to star in a series of low-budget films such as *Hercules*. Bill Bixby pursued a successful directing career, helming the subsequent Hulk movies and the popular *Blossom* television show, but he sadly passed away from prostate cancer in 1993.

Above and left: *Bill Bixby and Lou Ferrigno in publicity stills from the television show.* Below: *Lou Ferrigno makes a guest appearance in the feature film.*

MY HULK

I loved the old Hulk television show and it was a thrill to have Lou Ferrigno come and be a small part of our film. Back when the show was being made, a bodybuilder was the perfect solution. But, my Hulk has to be more than an embodiment of human strength. That is why this film could not be made without the help of the geniuses at ILM. We have approached the Hulk design from both the inside—with all the amazing ways they can create bone and muscle structure in the computer and then make it move—and also from the outside, taking inspirations from everything from Tibetan masks to the emotions we record on the face of his real-life co-stars. The Hulk has to perform opposite award-winning, amazingly gifted, and subtle talents. The key to the Hulk will be how good an actor he is. Our hope is that through computer animation, we can achieve the next generation of realism, that we can approach something that is haunting and emotional and not just a gimmick of computer work.

Ang Lee, Director

INVISIBLE TECHNOLOGY

Throughout my career, I've always followed the directors. It never really mattered whether or not they had worked on an effects film. We could always teach them the process and, on every film, we learn something new ourselves. We're always breaking new ground and I do really enjoy the thrill of discovery.

I couldn't turn down a chance to work with Ang Lee and to see what he would do with the Hulk. Usually, I am not that interested in a comic book story, per se, but

Animation director Colin Brady, visual effects supervisor Dennis Muren, and director Ang Lee check the monitors during the shoot. Behind them, F/X producer Tom Peitzman and Lori Arnold, ILM production manager, look on.

I find a story about people going through crisis really intriguing. Apparently, Ang saw something in the Hulk that nobody else saw and I wanted to find out what it was.

In our initial discussions, Ang talked about the scale of the Hulk and his feelings of torment as he transforms from Bruce into Hulk. What was the character going through? He has no control over the process but does he almost enjoy this physical expression of his emotions?

I was fascinated when Ang started talking about how all the molecular growth inside of the Hulk is tied into the universe. He talked about algae and lichen and blood cells and the galaxies and how there's some connection in the universe that makes everything work; a kind of yin/yang thing he wanted to get into the story of the Hulk. And the whole time I was thinking, "Wow! This could be really great!"

We had two choices on creating the Hulk: We could do it all CG (computer-generated) or make a film with a big actor going around knocking over miniature sets. Ang's vision was that the Hulk would be a fast-moving character, not this lumbering behemoth. He is going to move, almost as fast as he thinks, and that means he is defying gravity. We can obviously get a lot more realistic interaction with the other actors and the sets by creating the character with the latest computer graphics work. My choice is always to make something that is beyond what anyone has ever seen before and everyone agreed.

For me, the Hulk manifests the child in all of us; that time when we really couldn't control ourselves or our emotions. And even though he is a little bit child-

THE BEST IN THE WORLD

Dennis Muren and his team at Industrial Light and Magic are working with me. They have done everything from *Star Wars* to *Jurassic Park*. Working with them is like working with Yuen Woo Ping who helped me do the fighting in *Crouching Tiger, Hidden Dragon*. They are the best in the world, trying to do things they never thought they could accomplish before.

Ang Lee,
Director

13

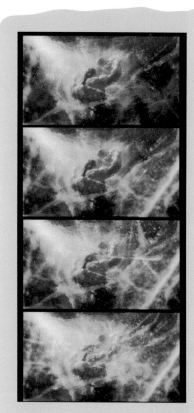

Concept drawing of the Hulk and his father under ice by Robert MacKenzie for a scene at the end of the movie. Below: Director Ang Lee on the set.

ish, he also has the same instincts as everybody. He just reacts a little bit faster and he is confused about where he is and what is going on. Why is this is happening to him? He doesn't think so much as he reacts.

All of these emotions have to come though his face and his body movements. The audience needs to recognize that he is like a child in this huge body. Our original ideas for the character came from everywhere. In the comics, the look of the Hulk keeps changing but we never thought we should make him look like a particular drawing in a particular story. I believe Marvel was really involved in the process, as was Ang and his production designer Rick Heinrichs, and in the end, they created something that is sort of a summary of the character.

At first we tried to mirror the original intent of the character with the strong green color on him. We had to back off on the green because it didn't seem to quite fit in the real world. Instead of that printed green from the comics, we made him more of an organic green. We needed to work on getting the light to bounce off him correctly. The Hulk has a sense of weight when he walks. If he sits down, he has to react with gravity. He's got to move like he's a real thing. In the end, he is not a monster, though he's not quite a person either. He is contemporary looking, in a very good way.

For every film we begin with storyboards. Here, though, Ang wanted to keep it loose until we got on the set. So we invented a computer program that could do

Top: *Storyboards depicting the scene where the Hulk battles the military in the desert cover the walls of the LA production office.* Below: *The statue of the Hulk, called a maquette and created by by Leo Rijn, shows the proportions of his body.*

real-time storyboards with motion. Ang got familiar with those and came up with some of the shots but, really, a lot of ideas came from the set. We shot the background plates with the actors acting to a big cardboard cutout of the Hulk's head. I was there to remind everyone how big the Hulk was going to be; where the eye line was and what should be moving around when he walks in front of something. For this film, that was our first look at the shots. Then we came back to ILM and started the process of making the monster in the computer; that took about four months.

Ang was pretty specific about the performances he wanted for both the Hulk's physical and facial movements. We didn't do any motion capture for the face but we needed a point of reference for every emotion. If, for example, the Hulk is kneeling down, talking to Jennifer, how is his face going to perform? Five different actors would perform that scene in five different ways and our job is to find the one that Ang wants for his leading actor. In the end, Ang was the best source in figuring out the little nuances of performance. He acted out the facial expressions for some of the scenes and we copied those expressions. Ultimately, Ang is actually going to be the Hulk. Why have anyone else do it?

Top: *Maquettes by Leo Rijn and an early proportional drawing of the Hulk.*

GIVING LIFE TO THE HULK

The maquette is really only the start of the process of giving life to the Hulk. His proportions and musculature are exaggerated but just within the realm of the familiar. Design-wise, it was clear that we had to make these exaggerations believable to the audience by focusing on the details. We had a bodybuilder pose for photographs and this reference kept us rooted in "real" anatomy while we pushed the Hulk's muscle performance into the realm of the fantastic. In essence, it was like forensic reconstruction in reverse, taking what he looked like in the static maquette, imagining his bones, muscles, tendons, veins, and then extrapolating from there. I give all the credit to ILM's team of talented CG sculptors for pulling off this daunting task.

Wilson Tang,
Visual Effects Art Director

It's incredibly difficult to make anything that even resembles a human out of an animated or computer-generated character because as we look at each other, we see hundreds of subtle body motions and each one provides information about the character. We've had to define those and apply them to the Hulk correctly to portray his childlike personality. We've got forty or fifty animators working on the character and they all have their own ideas about how to express emotion. However, we've got to make it appear as though there is only one Hulk actor, not all these animators. Everyone needs to be crystal clear about the intent of each scene and what attitude (or five attitudes) Ang wants in any given scene. This process takes a long, long time to pull together.

Nobody wanted this film to be about computer tricks; I have no interest in doing anything like that, I'm not even a computer guy. I am interested in telling a story and I care about the actors. My work is to react to the actors. When you are working on a film like this, you think about it as an audience member. You're thinking about the character of the Hulk and how he feels about Betty at this moment or about General Ross at that moment. The technology should be invisible. When the film is over, then you want the audience to say, "Wow, how did they even do that?"

Dennis Muren,
Visual Effects Supervisor

ANIMATING THE HULK

You can get away with a lot when you are creating a monster, an alien, or dinosaur. We've never seen a real version of any of these so we don't really know what they look like or how they move. But we see people every day and we are all experts on how people move. You have to be dead-on when you are trying to create a human character. If the eye direction is off just a little bit, if the blinks are a little bit too slow, it completely changes the character's attitude. More importantly, creating a believable human character is not just about the skin texture or the movement of the muscles, it's about portraying some sense of soul.

Animation on the Hulk is divided into two parts. The first part is the acting which includes face, body, and a rough muscle mass. The second part is an anatomy check, where a specialized team of 3D modelers and artists fix the broken areas and add muscle jiggle, skin sliding and wind in the hair. Primarily, I'm involved with Hulk's acting. Even though the audience is expecting a big green, angry guy, this is also a story about father and son.

In trying to create the Hulk, we would stomp around the office, pretending we're big heavy guys. We'd lift things up and throw them around, always over emphasizing certain motions. And Ang would say, "This isn't WWF Wrestling. This is real. If you're going to pick something up violently, just pick it up, don't play it for the camera." I was very surprised at how realistic he wanted to play the Hulk and so we always had to tone it down.

While we were shooting on the set, between takes, I'd take my video camera and pull Ang aside to have him act out some sequences. This is a very personal story for Ang and much of Ang shows up in the Hulk. Ang's movements would be very childlike, very frustrated, with a lot of imperfections. Hulk is not always coordinated; this is not a cartoon where he can just simply jump from here to there. Sometimes, he may slip and fall, especially when he first turns into the Hulk, early on in the film. He's not quite used to his big lumbering body. In the emotional scenes, Hulk is played very serious. The performance is intentionally muted, much like Chow Yun-Fat in *Crouching Tiger, Hidden Dragon*. This subtlety in acting direction is why I wanted to work with Ang. I don't think there's been a CG character yet that has been played this stoically. Of course when Hulk gets angry, subtly is thrown out the window. The Hulk-outs are pain, rage, and a little pleasure all mixed together. The intensity here is, I think, a nice contrast to Hulk's childlike side.

I believe Ang would be the first to say that we don't want to define the character as good or bad. And I think he likes walking that line. I see a lot of innocence in Hulk's character and what makes him work is playing up this childlike nature. He sees the world in a new way. Hulk is like a four-year-old kid, he gets frustrated, he throws tantrums. But he also enjoys his fits of rage, so you can't say he's completely

Darker lips #1

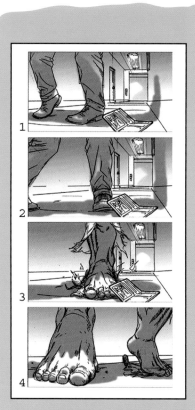

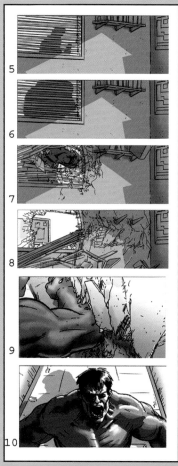

Above: *Maquette character designer Leo Rijn, director Ang Lee, and production designer Rick Heinrichs working in L.A. during the early stages of production.* Left: *In general, storyboards are created early in production, long before the film starts shooting. These storyboards, however, drawn by Brian O'Connell, were created much later in production for a re-shoot of a scene.*

innocent. He is also completely uninhibited; he's a person we'd all be, if we let our guard down.

Hulk is also a victim; he just wants to be left alone. He wouldn't start a fight. Ang would always say, "He's not a man killer, he doesn't want to kill people." Of course he is extremely violent; he could pick up a tank and throw it several miles but, at his core, he is really just a kid.

The most challenging shots are, strangely enough, the slow walks or any other action that involves subtle weight shifts. We have a pretty good handle on the close-ups and we can get away with a lot in the violent or supernatural sequences where, for example, the Hulk jumps three miles. Those are already kind of strange and magical moments. The tender moments are more difficult, especially when Hulk has to lift something up or get out of a chair. All animators are required to study video or motion capture.

Every single shot has some life reference. In fact, it's not so different from what they did on *Snow White* where they used a real actress who performed all of the dances and the movements; then they essentially copied her movements and exaggerated or changed them as necessary. I think somewhere along the way in the early years of computer graphics, they forgot that it all comes from real life, and they'd sit at their desk and think, okay, how is this character supposed to walk? Well, the best way to find out is to get out of your chair, go outside and start walking around and try a few different versions. Many of us get most inspired late at night, we go home and act out stuff in our living rooms

FOV: 98.2 Degrees
Aspect: 1.85
          VV.ACAD ANAM
Lens: 16 / 9.8 / 20

X.Y: 13.74, 2.51
Height: 133.9 Feet
Pitch   [360.1]
Yaw   [314.10]

Controls
Change Lens
Change Aspect
Set Camera Height
Adjust Camera Height
Toggle Help
Toggle Info

KEYS: Record Stop/Start = SPACE
       Play = P
       Snapshot = F9

Speed: 1

HELICAM: ON

Left: *Prior to production, ILM created a real-time, previz (pre-visualization) tool that allowed the director and crew members to get a better sense of how to shoot the Hulk in the real settings, even though the CG character did not yet exist. The tool resembles a video game using the character in CG versions of possible locations that help filmmakers plan their shoot in terms of composition and timing. Below: Storyboard by Mauro Borelli.*

or we go out in the parking lot and start throwing things around. That's really the core of it, even before we touch the computer.

Colin Brady,
Animation Director

BLOCKING

We started by looking at storyboards. We had a brilliant team of board artists and their drawings were kind of like comic books, but very inspired. We knew we had to strike those poses. Then we built mockups of the sets. On my laptop we built a low resolution, sort of video game version of the sets where we could block out the scene as if it was a stage play. We would hit all our cues and then know, roughly, the length of the scene. That was the first stake in the ground. Then we would show it to Ang who would say that Hulk is moving too much like a monster. "He has to move faster than that, at lightning speed sometimes."

And so we'd go back to the animators, and have them re-block the scene. It's very similar to blocking a theatrical performance.

Colin Brady,
Animation Director

THE PRODUCERS

A SHAKESPEAREAN TRAGEDY

We have been working on translating the Hulk to the big screen for more than a decade. The character appealed to me for many different reasons. I always thought the story of the Hulk, as presented in the Marvel Comics, had elements of a Shakespearean tragedy that had great cinematic potential. There was real, elemental drama of the human condition in this character. What I always liked about the Hulk was that he was not a superhero. The Jekyll and Hyde conflict intrigued me. Part of it is a cautionary tale, not only about the demons that we have to come to terms with inside ourselves, but it is also a bit of a commentary about the ramifications of having the technology to create a Hulk. The comic book dealt

Above: James Schamus, Avi Arad, Gale Anne Hurd, and Ang Lee on location during the shoot.

with Cold War issues, but we've been able to update it and it's relevant, if not more relevant, now.

We always had Ang Lee on our list of potential directors. So when Universal suggested it, Avi [Avi Arad, producer] and I felt that Ang would consider it because there is no more complex character than Banner/the Hulk. It's the ultimate split personality—two individuals that need to live with each other one way or another. They are tied in genetically, but they want to destroy each other and themselves at the same time. Looking at Ang's movies, I felt his keen interest in the inner soul, his sense of humor, his interest in family dynamics, in the relationships of fathers and sons, his inventive action in *Crouching Tiger;* he had all the ingredients to make a great movie.

Gale Anne Hurd, Producer

THE POPULAR HULK

Above: *Larry Franco and Avi Arad.*

Comic books are a reflection of the times we live in. They reflect our fears, social economics, wars, and so on. Marvel Comics first appeared in 1939 and, back then, people were concerned about gamma radiation, which was very misunderstood. The Hulk was a manifestation of the lack of understanding of what gamma rays can do.

Hulk didn't start as what you call run of the mill hero. Captain America is clearly a hero, he puts on the shield, he goes out and he saves people. Hulk was a deeper concept concerning the angst and the rage within us. He's about the guy, Bruce Banner, and he's about all of us.

We all know rage and our movie is dealing with the most universal reason for rage—childhood issues and memories and disappointments. The Hulk is not just a creature, he's a metaphor for something we all go through.

You know you won't like me when I'm angry.

The characters that endure are those to whom we can relate. Is there a human being on the planet who has never been afraid of their own anger? It happens to all of us. The Hulk reminds us that when we let the rage out, it can get pretty ugly.

Marvel Comics has published many different kinds of Hulk. Over the years we had a thinking Hulk, a talking Hulk, a smart Hulk, and so forth. Some of them were real dumb ideas but none of them affected Hulk's popularity.

People all over the world are realizing that movies based on Marvel heroes are not about the costume or the creature; they're about story and character. The audience is going to laugh, cry, cheer and be taken on a roller coaster ride that other movies can't provide. There's nothing more exciting or exhilarating than seeing a fifteen-foot creature take down a building. That's why we go to the movies.

Avi Arad, Producer

HIS HULKNESS

Unlike a lot of other superheroes, the Hulk is a superhero, a monster, and a person, and the various Hulk comics include the drama between generations of families, the quest for his origins, how he came to be who he is, the mystery of who he is...all of those things. We moved the script in those directions so that Ang could grapple with those ideas. More importantly, I think that Ang also sees the emotional, positive side of the Hulk. He understands that the Hulk isn't simply a monster that is there to scare us, but that everyone has the Hulk in them and there is something very enjoyable, very empowering about experiencing Hulkness. So, he was very interested in, for want of a better term, the entertainment side of the Hulk. He wanted to make it a very pleasurable experience, too.

James Schamus,
Screenwriter/Producer

THE CAST

ERIC BANA
BRUCE BANNER

JENNIFER CONNELLY
BETTY ROSS

NICK NOLTE
THE FATHER

JOSH LUCAS
TALBOT

SAM ELLIOTT
GENERAL ROSS

THE SCREENPLAY

"Oh soul, be changed to little water drops
And fall into the ocean, never be found."

— Marlowe, Doctor Faustus

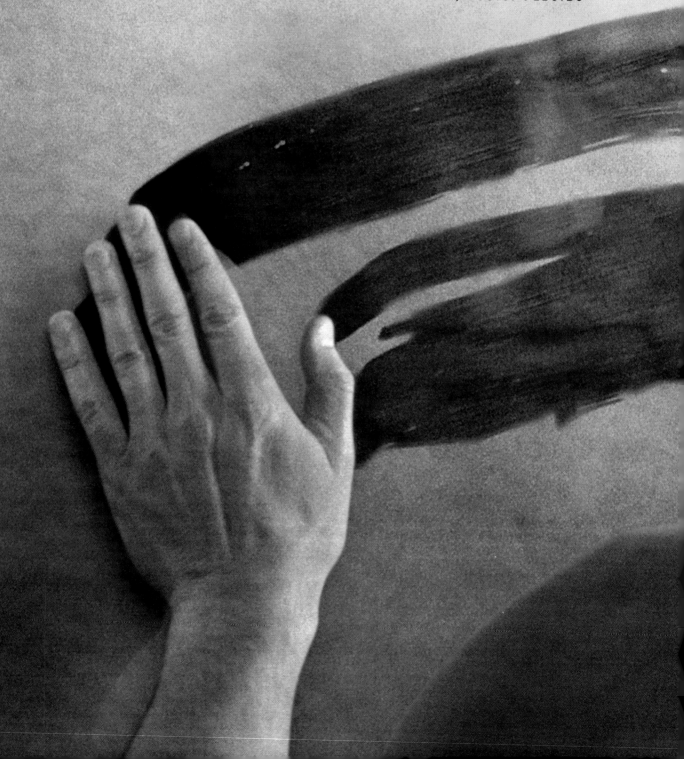

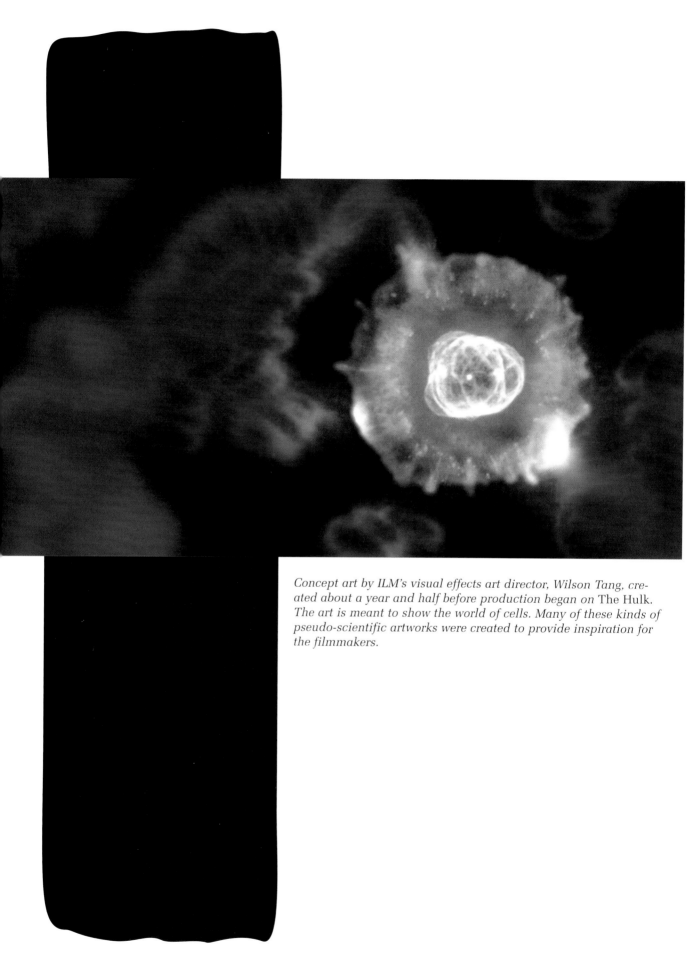

Concept art by ILM's visual effects art director, Wilson Tang, created about a year and half before production began on The Hulk. The art is meant to show the world of cells. Many of these kinds of pseudo-scientific artworks were created to provide inspiration for the filmmakers.

1965

INT. DESERT BASE — DAVID BANNER'S LAB — DAY

CREDIT SEQUENCE

Close-up: Cells, magnified under the lens of a microscope.

Dr. David Banner, thirties, looks up from the microscope, impassive.

Later: A baboon, inside a glass containment cage, is gassed, as David Banner, his hands inserted into sealed gloves, cradles its dying face.

1966: AMBITION

INT. DESERT BASE — ROSS'S OFFICE — DAY

> DAVID BANNER
> There is simply no practical way to shield against every weaponized agent. My approach will create super-immune systems—by strengthening the human cellular response—giving each cell its own chemical shield—

> ROSS
> Banner, I know where you're going—but manipulating the immune system, it's dangerous and stupid. I've told you a hundred times, and the president's science advisor has made it absolutely clear—no human subjects.

1967: SECRET KNOWLEDGE

INT. DESERT BASE — DAVID BANNER'S LAB — NIGHT

David Banner injects mutagenic agents into himself.

Later, alone in the lab, he studies his blood cells under a microscope.

1968: PATERNITY

INT. DESERT BASE — BANNER HOUSE — NIGHT

> EDITH BANNER
> David, I have wonderful news. I'm going to have a baby!

David Banner, trembling, stares back at her.

1969: AN ANIMAL CRY

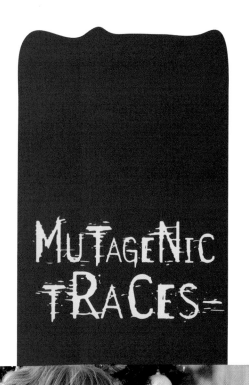

MUTAGENIC TRACES—

BUT OF WHAT ?

INT. DESERT BASE — HOSPITAL DELIVERY ROOM — DAY

The cries of Edith Banner, then the small cry of a baby—Bruce Banner is born.

1970: WATCHING

INT. PARENT'S HOUSE — DAY

The baby crawls, lifts himself up.

David Banner watches, takes the pacifier from its mouth.

The baby starts to scream, falls back, its joints distending oddly.

Banner studies him.

INT. DESERT BASE — BANNER HOUSE — NIGHT

Christmas. David Banner leans over his son, gives him two floppy cloth dolls.

Edith Banner watches in the background.

The boy takes them, laughs.

INT. DESERT BASE — BANNER HOUSE — DAY

David Banner draws blood into a syringe from the arm of his screaming son.

Edith surprises him in the doorway.

INT. DESERT BASE — LAB — NIGHT

David Banner smears the blood onto a glass plate, studies it under a microscope.

Close on: the cells.

Title:

MUTAGENIC TRACES — BUT OF WHAT?

INT. DESERT BASE — BANNER HOUSE — DAY

Mother at the kitchen table, sitting with a friend. Little Bruce runs in, expressionless, blood on the side of his face.

Title:

1973: INSTINCT

        EDITH BANNER
   Bruce, you're hurt.

Davey, another boy, runs in behind.

>   DAVEY
> Jack hit him with a stick, but Bruce
> wouldn't even hit him back. He just stood
> there, shaking and—

Bruce starts to shake again, his body distending. Then, with enormous effort, he calms, stops.

>   BRUCE BANNER
> It's OK.

INT. DESERT BASE — BANNER HOUSE — FAMILY ROOM — CONTINUOUS

A band-aid applied to little Bruce's face. He runs off.

>   FRIEND
> Strange, he hardly made a peep. Any
> other kid would've wailed his head off.

>   EDITH BANNER
>   (concerned)
> That's Bruce. He's just like that. He's just
> so—bottled up.

INT. DESERT BASE — ROSS'S OFFICE — DAY

>   ROSS
> The samples we found in your lab, they
> were human blood. You've ignored
> protocol.

>   DAVID BANNER
> You had no right, snooping around in my
> lab. That's my business!

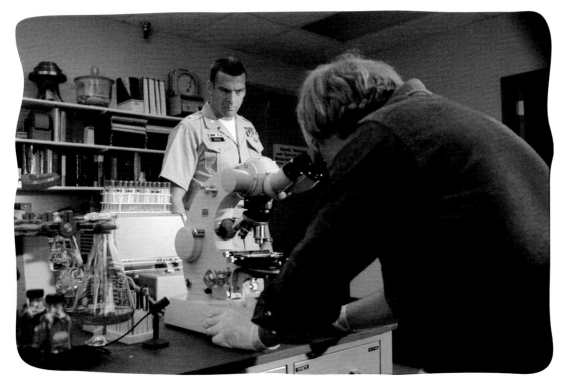

> ROSS
>
> Wrong Banner. It's government business.
> And you're off the project.

SABOTAGE

INT. DESERT BASE — CYCLOTRON ROOM — DAY

David Banner, shaking with rage, flips a series of switches.

INT. DESERT BASE — CYCLOTRON ROOM — DAY —
LATER

Banner strides down the hallway, as alarms begin to
sound.

INT. DESERT BASE — LAB — CONTROL ROOM —
CONTINUOUS

Alarm sounds continue.

> TECHNICIAN
>
> Attention all personnel, fail-safe has been
> initiated. Gamma decontamination will
> occur in thirty minutes. Evacuate immedi-
> ately. I repeat, evacuate immediately.

INT. DESERT BASE — BANNER HOUSE —
DAY

Little Bruce plays with his floppy dolls.
Alarms in background.

We hear his father enter the house, his
mother's voice rising.

We can't make out their words, but we can
feel the heat of their argument in the boy's
eyes.

His dolls: They morph into fighting monsters.

A flash: He looks up, amazed.

A scream.

INT. BRUCE'S ADOLESCENT BEDROOM — NIGHT

She flips on the light. Fourteen-year-old Bruce stares
blankly.

> MRS. KRENZLER
>
> Bruce. Bruce. Wake up, son. Bruce. Bruce.

> BRUCE
>
> I'm OK.

> MRS. KRENZLER
>
> Another nightmare.

> BRUCE
>
> I don't know. I don't remember.

INT. BRUCE'S BEDROOM — DAY

High school Bruce is on the floor, stacks of books spread around him, reading. He looks up as Mrs. Krenzler enters and sits beside him.

> BRUCE
> Hey, Mom.

> MRS. KRENZLER
> Already off to college. I'm going to miss you terribly.

> BRUCE
> I'll miss you, too.

> MRS. KRENZLER
> Please. Come here. Look at you, soon to be a great scientist.

> BRUCE
> I guess. I mean, who knows?

> MRS. KRENZLER
> I do. There's something inside you—so special—some kind of greatness, I am sure. Someday you're going to share it with the whole world.

EXT. BANNER'S HOUSE — BERKELEY — MORNING

To establish. Pleasant, residential.

INT. BANNER'S HOUSE — BATHROOM — MORNING

Bruce Banner, early thirties, handsome, intense, in front of the mirror, shaving. (He knows himself by the name of Bruce Krenzler—his adoptive name—but he'll soon learn his real one.)

The scrape of the razor.

Watching himself, in the mirror.

Scraping. Slow. The sound.

From inside the mirror, watching him—the eyes—do they seem different from his own?

He stops. Leans closer into the mirror, studying.

CLOSE UP

EXT. BERKELEY LAB

Bruce rides up on his bicycle, parks it in the bike rack and walks toward the entrance of the building. Two security guards pass by Bruce as he enters the building.

> SECURITY GUARD
> Morning, Dr. Krenzler.

SIGNING ON TO PLAY THE HULK

The most obvious hook for me in accepting this part was the fact that Ang Lee was directing it. The thing that attracted me to the character of the Hulk in particular was the fact that he is a slightly reluctant superhero. And the Hulk can't control being the Hulk, really—Batman goes into a cave, Superman goes into a phone booth, but it just comes over the Hulk, which attracted me as an actor.

Eric Bana, Actor

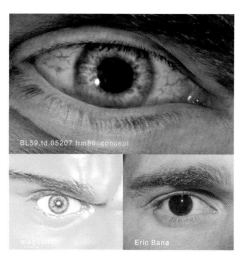

BL59.td.05207.frm80.concept

maquette   Eric Bana

Concept drawing by Wilson Tang (top) combines the elements of a human eye (bottom right) and the Hulk eye from the maquette (bottom left).

INT. BANNER'S LAB — HALLWAY

Bruce enters, hears:

> HARPER (O.S.)
> Bruce!

He is accosted at once by Harper. They move as they talk:

> HARPER (CONT'D)
> Big day. Did you sleep? I didn't sleep.

> BRUCE BANNER
> I slept OK. Is Betty here yet?

> HARPER
> She's around. I really gotta say, seeing you in that stylin' headwear...

> BRUCE BANNER
> (deadpan)
> You're implying something about my helmet.

ABOUT THE GREEN AND PURPLE

"Ang Lee seems to be a student of Western civilization and his interpretation of that, visually, was fascinating to me," says Rick Heinrichs, production designer. "He wanted to investigate these iconic images of America because, for Ang, I think there was something very Western, very American about the Hulk; men and their repressed anger and all that. Also, Lee wasn't interested in going specifically in one direction or another—finding equilibrium between apparent opposites attracted him. So, that was what we explored and it was quite a journey."

Of course, Heinrichs studied the Stan Lee/Jack Kirby comics, but this creative journey led him and Lee to a variety of other artists—from late nineteenth and early twentieth century American painters absorbing Impressionist and Oriental styles and colors, to the later Surrealist De Chirico, whose colors and illogical, dreamlike subjects attracted both the director and production designer. (What Heinrichs calls the De Chirico color palette appears predominantly in Bruce Banner's neighborhood and home.)

Heinrichs notes, "De Chirico was a painter who mainly worked in Europe, but there is a very Southwestern feel to his color palette—rusts, burgundies, yellows. There are some very strong hues and mellow ones mixed together and if you drive around the Berkeley Hills, you see this eclectic mix of colors. On our early scouts there, Ang would point out, 'Hey, there's a De Chirico.'"

Heinrichs favored another color combination, dubbed "the Krazy Kat palette."

"We also looked to the comic book artists of the early period. 'Krazy Kat' was a big influence. That was both in a selection of colors but also the concept—for instance, typically, you'll see a lit sky with a darker landscape, but if you study Krazy Kat, artist/illustrator George Herriman would switch that to a black sky with a lit landscape. We used that idea in a scene in the bathroom. We had a very dark color up above but a very light green tile below. There was something about that exchange I just loved. It turns you on your head a little bit and it's part of that duality, that tension between the light and the dark, between the simple and complex, the expected and the unexpected."

Heinrichs admits that the Hulk's signature colors also make appearances but, he hopes, not in an obvious way. Greens and purples were used as a nod to the comic book, and as a theme that follows Bruce Banner through his life.

HARPER
You look like a massive nerd. Even
around other scientists...
(pause/reaction from Banner)
Can I just ask—were you wearing the
helmet *while* she dumped you?

BRUCE BANNER
It protects my very important brain.
Go prep the samples.

BETTY ROSS (O.S.)
Found you!

Bruce turns to see Betty. She has a report in her hand, is
upset about something.

BRUCE BANNER
Betty. Hey.

He suddenly remembers his helmet, scrambles subtilely
to get it off while she fumes.

BETTY ROSS
I hate them!

BRUCE BANNER
I just got here. Who do we hate?

BETTY ROSS
The review board.
(holds the paper)
We've gotta make a presentation on
Tuesday...and you're gonna make it with
me.

BRUCE BANNER
You think I should?

BETTY ROSS
Yeah, you're great with that stuff...Start
talking about microbes and nanomeds,
you sound almost...passionate.

He tries not to look hurt.

BRUCE BANNER
(tries...)
Nobody expects this to be easy. Working
together, after we were...so close...

BETTY ROSS
We were close?

BRUCE BANNER
(so bad at this talk)
If I could...be different, open up or
whatever, I...

BETTY ROSS
Don't. It's not your fault. You're just a
by-product of my inexplicable obsession

Science advisor John Underkoffler helped to guide Lee, the
cast, and the crew through the
intricate vagaries of the science
that might create a Hulk and, in
the process, the director
learned to appreciate the pure
artistry of the miniscule forms
that led to such an immense
monster. Underkoffler primarily
made sure that the story was
rooted in accurate science and
that the jargon was at least
based in reality.

According to Underkoffler,
"The first thing they wanted me
to come up with was an expla-
nation for the research that the
scientists in the film were pur-
suing, which would then lead to
the accident that creates the
Hulk. Lee also wanted all the
background, the techniques and
gestures—from how to hold a
beaker to the more theoreti-
cal—to be as realistic as possible. Audiences are increasingly
savvy about this stuff even if the
general audience may not have
much familiarity with this argot,
it recognizes when the rhythms
are authentic."

In that spirit, Underkoffler
gave the actors a crash course
in science and accompanied Lee
and the principal cast to Cal
Tech in advance of principal photography. He also met with the
actors and worked with them
on the background for their
characters, including their edu-
cation, their career trajectory
and their specific scientific disci-
pline. While at Cal Tech, the
actors received hands-on train-
ing with laboratory equipment
and observed research scientists in their day-to-day routines.

with emotionally distant men. I'll get over us.

> BRUCE BANNER
> (very softly)
> Good for you.

It's clear he doesn't want her to get over them, but not clear to her.

> BETTY ROSS
> Anyway, I'm just really stressed about this review. If we don't get impressive results today, we're gonna have a hard sell come Tuesday.

He smiles, reassuringly—brave face to bury their talk.

> BRUCE BANNER
> Then let's go be impressive.

INT. BANNER'S LAB — GAMMA ROOM — DAY

The frog sits inside a transparent chamber of thick glass, surrounded by the glittering panels of a gammasphere.

> BRUCE BANNER (V.O.)
> Harper, release the nanomeds.

A hissing sound, the chamber fills with gas.

> BRUCE BANNER (CONT'D)
> OK, let's hit Freddie with the gamma radiation.

Harper, slightly seedy lab assistant, punches instructions into a keyboard.

A pinpoint of gamma radiation hits a focal lens above the pedestal. In a flash, it zaps the frog across its chest.

The ugly gash.

For a moment, nothing.

Bruce Banner, watching.

Slowly, the wound begins, miraculously, to close up. As it closes, it leaves a zone of throbbing, almost fluorescent green in its wake, the freshly-pro-duced tissue saturated with color.

Next to Banner, Betty Ross, late twenties/early thirties, beautiful, smart.

> BETTY ROSS
> (under her breath)
> Yes.

But suddenly: Splat! The frog explodes, splashing its innards all over the inside of the con-tainer.

Disappointment. Banner, tense.

INT. LAWRENCE BERKELEY LAB — BANNER'S LAB — NIGHT

Bruce and Betty are in the lab, working the problem but also kicking back and celebrating their failure. They've got a couple of beers, are fairly casual.

Concept drawing by Wilson Tang of the sequence where the frog explodes during a lab experiment early in the film.

> BRUCE BANNER
> (looking up)
> You wanna go to the review board on Monday and tell them we've developed a brand new method for exploding frogs?

> BETTY ROSS
> (playful)
> Yeah, I think maybe there's a market for it. What if there's a plague?

> BRUCE BANNER
> (smiling)
> What have you had, like one beer?

> BETTY ROSS
> I'm just saying…frogs start falling from the sky…who do they come to? We'd be world renowned.

> BRUCE BANNER
> Make any parent proud.

Her smile becomes a contemplation of him. After a beat:

> BETTY ROSS
> I bet they would be.

> BRUCE BANNER
> They wanted me to be a pilot.

ABOUT BETTY

There's something kind of vulnerable about Betty Ross, something missing, something slightly broken about her. Her relationship with Bruce is complicated. They had a romantic relationship, which did not work out—but they are still professional partners. And Betty is still very much in love with Bruce.

Betty recognizes, even before the accident, the effect that anger, or rather the suppression of anger, has on Bruce. And then she is the first one to sense and piece together what's going on after the accident. She recognizes that in the Hulk. She recognizes Bruce and stands her ground. Others respond with an escalation of violence, but Betty stands there in front of him and looks at him as if to say, "I'm here, I understand, I love you and I see you…and it's going to be OK."

Jennifer Connelly, Actress

> BETTY ROSS
> I mean your birth parents.

> BRUCE BANNER
> I guess we'll never know.

> BETTY ROSS
> I don't understand why you don't want to find out about them.

> BRUCE BANNER
> They're dead. They died before I remember anything and why do you always come back to this?

> BETTY ROSS
> I guess I figure there's more to you than you like to show. I guess there couldn't be any less.

> BRUCE BANNER
> And, we come full circle back to that….
> Nice work, Betty.

EXT. LAWRENCE BERKELEY LAB — DAY

As Betty enters, she hears a voice calling from behind her.

> TALBOT
> Betty!

> BETTY ROSS
> Glenn?

INT. LAWRENCE BERKELEY LAB — BANNER'S LAB — DAY

> BETTY ROSS
> What happened to your uniform?

> TALBOT
> I switched over. Still work with your dad, but, you know, the military's subcontracting out all the most interesting work, and I can't argue with the paycheck. I basically run all the labs on the base now. (He gives her a quick look-over.) Hey, you're looking good.

Talbot and Betty enter lab.

> Ah, the good 'ole college days.
> (pause)
> So how's business?

> BETTY
> What do you want?

He smiles, ingratiatingly.

> TALBOT
> OK, I'll cut to the chase. I've been hearing

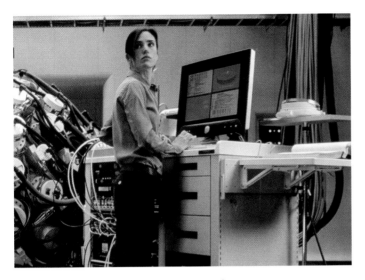

interesting things about what you guys are doing here. This could have some significant applications. How'd you like to come work for Atheon, get paid ten times as much as you now earn, and own a piece of the patents?

She rises.

                BETTY ROSS
              (pointing)
    Glenn, two words: the door.

At which moment, the door opens, and Banner enters. He stops, sizing up the situation.

INT. DESERT BASE — ROSS'S OFFICE — NIGHT

Ross, sits at his desk. An aide comes in with a folder.

                AIDE
    General. Talbot wanted you to see this.
    It's about a lab Atheon is targeting for
    acquisition and removal to desert base.

                ROSS
    Why isn't he going through NSC?

                AIDE
    It concerns your daughter, sir.

INT. LAWRENCE BERKELEY LAB — HALLWAY — NIGHT

The slow, almost unsteady movement of a janitor's cart, being pushed tiredly.

It stops. A bucket, dirty water, a mop.

Powerful hands slowly mop the floor, back and forth.

The janitor's eyes, distant.

We'll call him, simply, "The Father."

CASTING NICK NOLTE

Nick is an actor's actor. He is generous and fearless with everyone and is a great spirit. He immediately saw connections in the film between popular Western culture and Eastern philosophy that I didn't even see.

Ang Lee, Director

We don't see The Father's face in its entirety, but it's vaguely familiar.

He stops, leans against the mop, listens—he's standing in front of the door to Banner's lab.

Muffled voices.

INT. LAWRENCE BERKELEY LAB — HALLWAY — NIGHT

Betty passes by the janitor.

She feels his gaze on her back as she walks down the hall, stops, turns around.

> BETTY ROSS
> Hey, um, what happened to Benny? Is he still working the night shift?

> FATHER
> Benny's dead. I'm the new guy.

> BETTY ROSS
> Oh. Glad to meet you.

> FATHER
> Same.

He moves down the hall.

INT. LAWRENCE BERKELEY LAB — BANNER'S OFFICE — NIGHT

Banner, working.

Pauses, takes out a snapshot from his desk drawer: Betty and he, sitting in front of a cabin in the woods, a lake behind them.

Close on the photo: the sound of the wind in the trees, the color saturates, comes alive.

Title:

MEMORY

DESIRE

EXT. REDWOOD CABIN — DAY

The camera, on a timer, clicks. Banner gets up to reset it.

>   BRUCE BANNER
> Let's try another.

>   BETTY ROSS
> No, I look tired.

>   BRUCE BANNER
> You are tired, but you look great.

He resets the camera. Then goes to sit beside her. He puts her arms around her; the camera takes the picture.

He looks at her. Brushes her hair back.

>   BRUCE BANNER (CONT'D)
> Hey. What's the matter?

>   BETTY
> It's the dreams, they're terrible. I keep
> having them.

>   BANNER
> Then do like me—don't sleep.

>   BETTY
> Not an option, and it shouldn't be for you
> either.

>   BANNER
> Tell me about your dream.

>   BETTY
> It starts as a memory—I think it's my first
> memory. An image I have from when I
> was maybe two years old.

INT. ICE CREAM PARLOR — DAY

Flashback:

A little girl, laughing, being lifted and thrown from her father's arms, and caught, and thrown again. Her father, in military uniform—we see him from behind.

A Jeep pulls up outside, soldiers beckon, the officer puts the girl down, she starts to cry.

The sky darkens, a low menacing rumble.

FATHERS AND SONS

I read the comic years ago but I wasn't a particular fan. When Ang came out to the house, we sat down and talked. He said, "I don't know how to make a comic book but I can make a great tragedy." That was interesting to me because it meant we could explore the darkness of the father/son relationship, the responsibility of becoming what one is, the constant play between what we consider our conscious good side and our unconscious dark side and the integration of the shadow side of our personality into the light of day.

Nick Nolte, Actor

In the distance, an enormous dust cloud, some kind of bomb.

Various shots: the dusty streets of the base, as the cloud rises. A glimpse of a young boy's face, looking through the window of one of the small houses at the darkening sky—Banner?

EXT. REDWOOD CABIN — DAY

> BANNER
> You think it's a dream or a memory?

> BETTY
> I think it's something that must have happened out at Desert Base, with my father. Anyhow, the dream goes on and suddenly I'm alone.

FLASH BACK

INT. ICE CREAM PARLOR — DAY

The girl cries and cries.

Then:

A hand covers the girl's mouth. She looks up in terror. A man, his face obscured by the sun behind him.

Her eyes, widening.

We make out his features:

Banner, grim, determined.

EXT. REDWOOD CABIN — DAY

Back to the present. Banner is chagrined.

> BANNER
> But that's terrible. You know I would
> never hurt you.

> BETTY
> (affectionate, but pained)
> You already have.

> BANNER
> How?

> BETTY
> You're breaking my heart.

INT. LAWRENCE BERKELEY — BANNER'S OFFICE —
NIGHT

Banner puts down the photo, picks up his bag and exits.

INT. BERKELEY LAB — HALLWAY — NIGHT

He walks into the main hallway—deserted, a few lights on,
some evening light drifting in.

He hears a whimper from around a corner.

He walks toward the sound.

More whimpering.

He turns a corner. A small,
mangy-looking poodle sits
in the middle of the hallway,
alone.

> BANNER
> Hey there, who are
> you?

He goes to pet it. Suddenly,
it bares its rotten teeth and
growls, snapping.

> BANNER (CONT'D)
> OK. OK.

Banner backs away, looking
around for the dog's owner,
nowhere to be found.

INT. LAWRENCE BERKELEY LAB — BANNER'S OFFICE
— NIGHT

The janitor's cart.

Banner's office chair. The Father's hand, rubbing along it, finds a hair, picks it up, holds it up to the light.

EXT. BERKELEY HILLS STREETS — NIGHT

Banner speeds down the hill on his bike.

EXT. BERKELEY HILLS STREETS — CONTINUOUS

Banner, now going up a hill.

His legs, straining.

His eyes.

EXT. BANNER'S HOUSE — NIGHT

Banner rides up on bicycle

INT. BANNER'S HOUSE — LIVING ROOM — NIGHT

Banner sits at a makeshift desk. He absentmindedly tends a small Zen moss garden on the desktop.

Later: A scratchpad — figures, calculations, sketches, DNA sequences. Data sheets lying about.

The clock: 2:27 a.m.

Banner gets up from his work. Stands at the window.

Shadows from a willow tree, light from a street lamp, an intricate, dancing web.

EXT. BANNER'S HOUSE — NIGHT

On the sidewalk in front of the house, under the willow tree, a single figure walks. He pauses. We see him only in silhouette: tall, powerful, but slightly stooped. He stands there, sinister, looking up at the house.

The willow's shadows bend. They seem to form a pattern, subtly, like a Rorschach or a subliminal M. C. Escher engraving, two interlocked faces—the faces of a pair of distorted stuffed animals, the dolls from Banner's childhood.

INT. BANNER'S HOUSE — BEDROOM — NIGHT

Inside:

Later, Banner sitting up in bed, cross-referencing more data sheets, taking notes. He throws the pencil down.

           BANNER
   Damn.

Title:

IN DREAMS, THE KNOWLEDGE HE SEEKS

ARE MEMORIES HE CANNOT GRASP

Later: Banner sits, somnolent.

His breathing.

The clock: 4:48.

His eyes, starting to flutter closed. A haunting, echoing sound of footsteps, the sound of the whimpering dog.

Bruce's closing eyes. Beneath the eyelids, rapid movements—dream state.

INT. SMALL HOUSE — NEW MEXICO — 1973 — DAY

Images sweep over the screen, as in a dream, barely coherent:

A small boy, four years old, plays with a pair of stuffed toys—long beaks, floppy ears, oversized feet.

His small hands, lifting the toys into the air, flying them down.

He makes noises—small shouts of surprise, sound effects, crashes, skids.

His POV: As he moves the toys about, they become slightly, almost indistinguishably more animated. We hear voices—adult, human voices, a man and a woman, in the background, but can't make out what they say, only that their voices rise to a fevered pitch.

Yelling.

And then, an unearthly, primal scream.

It emerges from the boy's mouth.

IN DREAMS, THE KNOWLEDGE HE SEEKS ARE MEMORIES HE CANNOT GRASP

CUT TO:

EXT. BANNER'S HOUSE — NIGHT

The same scream, muffled, coming from inside.

INT. BANNER'S HOUSE — BEDROOM — CONTINUOUS

Banner, startled, rising from the bed.

His eyes.

Something catches his attention out the window.

The lone figure, still there, in the shadows. Obscured, but seeming to look up at him.

Banner—pulls the blinds closed, breathes in deep, then opens the blinds again—but now, only shadows.

EXT. STREET — NIGHT

The figure walks away. Behind him trail three ill-kept dogs; a mastiff, a pit bull, and the poodle we saw earlier.

EXT. FATHER'S HOUSE — OAKLAND — NIGHT

The small, weedy yard of a run-down row house, chain link fence.

The Father unlocks a padlock on the gate. The dogs run in ahead of him.

CASTING THE HULK

Eric Bana played a kind of human monster in *Chopper*, someone who was so monstrous because he was so human, too. With just a simple look, he could communicate a kind of superhuman fury and intelligence. I thought it would be marvelous to see him as Bruce Banner, having to suppress that energy until he couldn't take it anymore.

Ang Lee, Director

He throws them strips and chunks of meat and old vegetables, then unlocks and enters the house.

INT. FATHER HOUSE — NIGHT

Light from a single bulb—the place just about as you'd expect. Dirty, a mattress in a corner, not much of anything else. Except: on a long worn table, stacks of papers, books, journals, and a small work area. The man clears a pile, under which is a gleaming, super thin notebook computer. He opens the screen, presses a button, and sits down.

The light from the screen illuminates his face—and now we recognize him: Dr. David Banner, thirty years older.

On the wall behind the computer screen, a bulletin board, filled with images and clippings: various scenes from Bruce Banner's career, yearbook photos, graduation, etc.

The Father's face, pensive. He raises a hand, touches one of the photos.

FATHER
Bruce. My Bruce.

From a small container, The Father pulls out the strand of hair.

He places it on a glass plate. Chops it into tiny fine pieces with a razor. Puts the pieces into a small test tube filled partway with a milky substance, then puts the test tube inside an apparatus which will culture the DNA from the hair.

Title: HIS SON'S DNA—STILL—A MYSTERY

The apparatus hums and vibrates. A wire runs to the super thin notebook computer.

From behind, we hear him tap remarkably quickly on the keypad.

INT. LAWRENCE BERKELEY LAB — BANNER'S LAB — DAY

Banner enters—to discover Talbot and Betty talking.

BETTY ROSS
Morning. Glenn stopped by—

BRUCE BANNER
What's he doing here?

TALBOT
You know, Dr. Krenzler, we've never had the chance to get to know each other properly.

BRUCE BANNER
That's because I don't want to get to know you, properly or improperly. Leave.

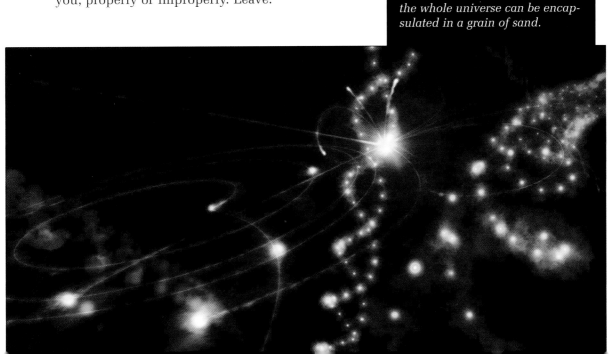

Concept art by Wilson Tang showing the world of cells. According to Tang, Ang Lee asked him to show the idea that the whole universe can be encapsulated in a grain of sand.

ABOUT TALBOT

Talbot is incredibly driven, extremely ambitious, powerful, self-righteous and ruthless. He is a military-trained, disciplined human being who truly believes that he is exalted and that his ideas are going to transform the world and, therefore, he has a right and a duty to achieve them by any means necessary. He is the type who believes that his political and sociological ideologies are so correct that they will do anything to fulfill their own prophecy.

He is so crazily free, so maniacal, unafraid, and dominating that there is this great comic book element to him. I'm not a particularly antagonistic person, but everyone has some hostility or aggression inside, which, I suppose, is one of the points of *The Hulk*. I don't get to release those elements of my personality on a daily basis and often, as an actor, it's easier to play characters that are further away from your normal life. It was almost playful to portray Talbot and absolutely fun. He's also a terrific foil for Banner, who is so obviously suppressed.

Josh Lucas, Actor

TALBOT
(smarmy)
Hey, no worries.

He goes to the doorway, out of earshot of Betty, then turns—nose to nose with Banner.

TALBOT (CONT'D)
But let me give you a little heads up. There's a hair's breadth between friendly offer and hostile takeover. I've done my homework. The stuff you're doing here is dynamite. Think: GIs imbedded with technology that makes them instantly repairable on the battlefield, in our sole possession. That's a hell of a business.

BRUCE BANNER
That's not what we're doing here. We're doing the basic science, for everyone—

TALBOT
You know, someday I'm going to write a book. I'm gonna call it, "When Stupid Ideals Happen to Smart Penniless Scientists." In the meantime, Bruce, you'll be hearing from me.

INT. LAWRENCE BERKELEY LAB — GAMMA ROOM — DAY

Later. Experiment in process.

Harper, at his monitoring station: countdown in progress.

BETTY ROSS
About Glenn, I...

BRUCE BANNER
There's nothing to talk about.

Banner pauses. In the corner of his eye he watches Harper through the glass window, wedged in the center of the gammasphere, testing the interlock switch.

BETTY ROSS
OK, just wanted to say don't worry about him. I'll handle it.

BRUCE BANNER
How?

BETTY ROSS
I'll call my father. Ask him to exert some pressure.

BRUCE BANNER
Last I heard, you and your father weren't speaking.

BETTY ROSS
Now I have something to talk with him about.

Harper calls out through the intercom.

HARPER (V.O.)
(over intercom)
Um, I think the circuit kind of fried, or, I don't know, maybe you want to take a look.

THE GAMMASPHERE

The original Hulk comic book tale has a specific element of science built in, namely the gamma radiation that transforms Bruce Banner into the Hulk. However, for the movie, director Ang Lee wanted something that went beyond the 1950s notions about radiation and the cliché monster results of exposure.

As in the comic book, a toxic dose of gamma rays penetrates Bruce Banner in an experiment that goes awry. For Ang's film, the culprit is now a dome-like structure with colorful green, yellow, and red pods dotting its circumference, known as the gammasphere. While the gammasphere's functions in the film are fictional, the object is inspired by the real and only one housed at the University of California at Berkeley.

"Ours was almost an exact visual duplicate of the real one at the Lawrence Berkeley lab, although it weighed a lot less," explains John Underkoffler who acted as science advisor on the film. "When Ang Lee and [production designer] Rick Heinrichs visited Berkeley, they saw this fantastic object that was designed for sensitive experiments. It happens to be an amazingly beautiful object that is very cinematic, with such vivid colors and those angled metal supports, it seemed as though it was designed for us. So, we incorporated it into the movie, thanks to the help of the folks at the Lawrence Berkeley lab."

BRUCE BANNER
OK. I'll be right there.

Banner goes into the experiment area, picking up a respirator mask.

He's just entering the clean room, mask in hand, when the interlock switch—Harper's still fiddling with it—shorts out. There's a few sparks.

Flashing lights and a quiet audio countdown klaxon resume in the clean room.

Inside the gammasphere, Harper tries to back out, but his mask catches on one of the protruding alignment rods. He panics. Bruce sprints over to him, reaches in, pulls the snagged mask free.

In the control room, Betty has moved to Harper's work station. The control software on his monitor is no longer paused. She tries to stop the countdown, but there's no response to the keyboard.

BETTY ROSS
Bruce! The interlock!

At the gammasphere halves, Bruce hurls the freed Harper backward. Harper secures his mask, just as the countdown reaches zero. The nanomeds release, as the gamma canisters rotate into armed position.

Betty: pounding on the glass. We can't hear her from inside the chamber, as she screams for Banner to get out.

Bruce realizes that Harper and Betty are directly in the line of fire. With one second left, he makes his decision. He turns back to the sphere, raises his arms, and blocks the opening.

The gamma canisters fire. He takes the full blast. His body glows with the radiant energy.

Alarms sound.

Banner lets out a hideous yell.

Close: Banner's face.

Flash: the floppy dolls, morphing.

Flash: the bomb in the desert.

Banner drops to his knees, we hear pounding on the door to the isolation chamber.

Oddly, there is a small smile on his face.

INT. INFIRMARY — EXAM ROOM — DAY

Banner is sitting alone in bed, almost gleeful.

The door pops open, Betty rushes in anxious. Closed door behind her.

>   BRUCE BANNER
> How's Harper?

Betty pulls a chair next to the bed and sits down.

>   BETTY ROSS
>   (worried)
> He's alright. You saved him. I don't think
> he's coming back to the lab for a while.
>   (Betty shaking)
> I don't understand. How is this possible?
> You should be dead.

>   BRUCE BANNER
> They worked. The nanomeds, they—I feel
> great. I feel like they, I don't know, fixed
> me.

>   BETTY ROSS
> Bruce...the nanomeds have killed every-
> thing they've come in contact with. Are
> you sure the doctor checked you?

The gammasphere plays an important role in the storyline and was modeled on a real machine in the Lawrence Berkeley lab. The big difference is that the movie gammasphere is meant to emit gamma rays while the real one detects them. Machined from aluminum, the Hulk gammasphere measured about eight feet in height and width.

> BRUCE BANNER
> (laughs a bit)
> He did the full work-up, he wants to know where he can get what I'm taking. I'm a hundred percent.
> (pause)
> More.

> BETTY ROSS
> What do you mean?

> BRUCE BANNER
> You remember my bad knee? Well, now it's my good knee.

> BETTY ROSS
> Bruce, this isn't funny.
> (tears up)
> I was watching! You were gonna die and I was gonna have to watch you die.

She struggles to get control of herself. He reaches out to her.

> BRUCE BANNER
> I'm sorry. Really...hey...I'm not going to explode.

She rolls her eyes, even through tears.

> BRUCE BANNER (CONT'D)
> You should get some rest...I'm fine. Really, I've never felt better.

INT. INFIRMARY — BANNER'S ROOM — NIGHT

Banner, sitting up in a hospital bed, hooked up to various monitors.

The monitors: nothing abnormal.

He picks up the phone, dials.

> BRUCE BANNER
> Hey.

> BETTY ROSS
> Hey. How are you?

> BRUCE BANNER
> I'm fine.

> BETTY ROSS
> You sure?

> BRUCE BANNER
> Yeah.

> BETTY ROSS
> What are you doing?

                    BRUCE BANNER
I was just sitting here, thinking, about
you, about your dream.

                    BETTY ROSS
What dream?

                    BRUCE BANNER
In the desert.

                    BETTY ROSS
And what were you thinking about?

                    BRUCE BANNER
I don't know. Sometimes, when I'm
not really thinking about much of
anything, I remember images from
it. Did I ever tell you that?

                    BETTY ROSS
No.

                    BRUCE BANNER
It's as if I dreamed it myself.

                    BETTY ROSS
You should get some sleep.

                    BRUCE BANNER
Yeah. You, too.

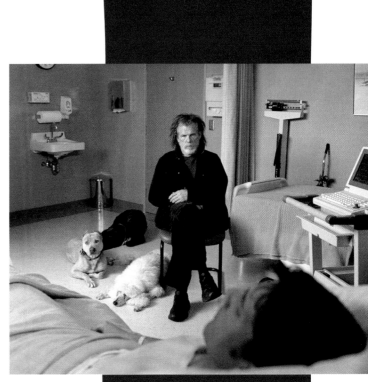

Time passes.

Banner nods off.

A whimpering sound, a slight growl.

He opens his eyes. The lamplight from the parking lot
spills in through the window, dreamlike. He sees:

Sitting across the room, surrounded by his dogs—The
Father.

Banner sits up as the dogs lift their heads, purr.

The Father just sits, silently, almost kindly.

Banner—senses The Father's kinship, instinctive familiarity, nervous and wary of the dogs, the intruder's presence.

                    FATHER
Your name is not Krenzler. It's Banner.

                    BRUCE BANNER
What?

                    FATHER
Your name. It's Banner, Bruce Banner.
Bruce.

                    BRUCE BANNER
How did you get in here?

Flash: The Father, thirty years younger, handsome, hold-

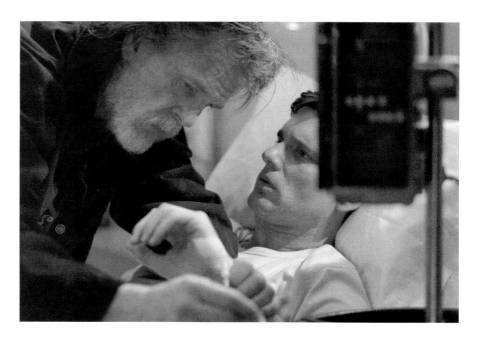

ing the stuffed animals, offering them as a gift, smiling.

> FATHER
> I work here now, in the labs. The late
> shift. It keeps me close to you. You
> always work so late yourself, with your
> friend, Miss Ross.

Banner starts to sit up, but gets tangled in wires, tubes.

> FATHER (CONT'D)
> No, please. You're not well.

He goes to Banner, unsorts the jumble as he talks.

> FATHER (CONT'D)
> You've had an accident. You're wondering
> why you're still alive, aren't you? You're
> thinking: There's something inside, some-
> thing different, inexplicable. I can help
> you understand, if you'll let me, if you'll
> forgive me.

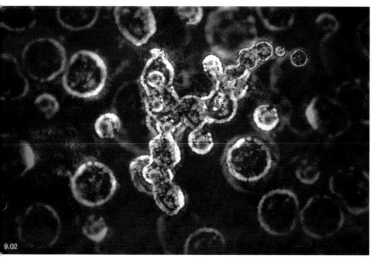

*Concept art by Wilson Tang of cell
mutation within the body.*

> BRUCE BANNER
> Look, mister, I'm sure I have noth-
> ing to forgive you for. So, maybe
> you'd better just go. Please. I'll be
> fine.

> FATHER
> You must know. You don't want to
> believe it, but I can see it in your
> eyes—so much like your mother's.
> Of course, you're my flesh and
> blood—but then, you're something
> else, too, aren't you? My physical
> son, but the child of my mind, too.

BRUCE BANNER
You're lying. My parents died when I was
a small boy.

FATHER
That's what they wanted you to believe.
The experiments, the accident—they
were top secret. They put me away, thirty
years—away from you, away from our
work—but they couldn't keep me forever.
After all, I'm sane. They had to admit it.

The Father raises his arm. The dogs come to attention.

FATHER (CONT'D)
You see, everything your extraordinary
mind has been seeking, all these years—
it's been inside of you—and now we will
understand it, harness it—

The phone rings. Banner looks over to it.

FATHER (CONT'D)
Miss Ross, again. Don't answer! There's
something you need to know about her,
Bruce, something troublesome—but I can
protect you from her.

In a flash, Banner starts to tremble.

BRUCE BANNER
You're crazy! Get out!

A look of menacing hatred passes over The Father's face.
The dogs crouch for an attack.

BANNER
Get. Out.

FATHER
(to the dogs)
Heel.

The dogs back off. A pregnant pause.

FATHER (CONT'D)
We're going to have to watch that temper
of yours.

He goes. The dogs follow.

INT. INFIRMARY — LATER:

Banner, asleep, dreaming, thrashing in bed.

Flash: the gamma explosion.

Under the sheets, his body groans, stretches. Tubes pop
out.

The bed depresses.

53

INSPIRATION

As far as inspiration, Ang and I went all the way back to the very earliest renderings of Hulk and his story, set in the early 1960s. We had over forty years of riches to draw from. Many different people wrote and penned these stories and there are many different versions of the Hulk; there are green Hulks and gray Hulks and green Hulks fighting gray Hulks. So we had to make a crucial decision as to where we were going to plant our flag. We didn't want to go backwards and simply rehash something from another medium and era. On the other hand, we bore the weight of many competing traditions that we didn't want to subvert or destroy in the process. In the end, we found a wealth of psychological and emotional back story that we eventually transformed into something new which we feel confident represents the essence of the Hulk.

James Schamus,
Screenwriter/Producer

Ang Lee and cinematographer Fred Elmes setting up a shot on location.

Around his eyes, is it the reflection of a street light, or is there a tinge of green?

He bolts awake in a cold sweat.

In the darkness, he stumbles. We hear the crash of a lamp falling.

Banner, still in the darkness, makes his way to the bathroom.

INT. LAWRENCE BERKELEY LAB — INFIRMARY — BATHROOM — CONTINUOUS

A flash—Banner has turned on the mirror light. He studies himself in the mirror. Nothing.

Camera pulls back: we see—the stitching on his T-shirt and pajama legs — ripped at the seams.

His eyes: afraid.

They close. He collapses.

EXT. FATHER HOUSE — NIGHT

In the shadows, The Father's dogs circle, silent, nervous.

INT. FATHER HOUSE — NIGHT

Containers of various sizes, marked with various warning stickers (all stolen from Banner's lab), litter the room.

From under a table, The Father picks up a cage—a large rat scurries inside. He places the cage inside another clear container in the middle of the room, and drops one of the canisters inside. It's the same type of canister from which the nanomeds were released in the earlier experiments.

He goes into the hallway, stands around the corner, and flips a light switch.

The room is immediately alive with the hum of radiation. The rat's cage starts to spark. The canister breaks open. A cloud envelops the rat, and then, one last spark, and The Father turns off the juice.

Gingerly, he turns the corner, back into the room, looks at the cage.

Inside, the rat—open sores, burns, slimy—but now three times as big, frothing, tearing at the cage.

The Father smiles.

INT. LAWRENCE BERKELEY LAB — BANNER'S OFFICE— DAY

Betty is taking blood from Banner. She finishes taking the blood.

BETTY ROSS
You sure you're OK?

BRUCE BANNER
Sure. How are you?

BETTY ROSS
I got a message from my father. He's coming to see me.

BRUCE BANNER
Your father? When?

BETTY ROSS
He lands in an hour. Funny thing was, he called me.

INT. LAWRENCE BERKELEY LAB —
BANNER'S LAB — MONTAGE

The vial.

Banner tests it.

Microscope.

The day passes.

Computer.

Frustration.

Title: MUTAGENIC TRACES—BUT OF WHAT?

EXT. JOINT TACTICAL FORCE WEST — GUARD GATE

Betty drives onto the base, shows her ID to a guard at the gate.

INT. JOINT TACTICAL FORCE WEST — OFFICERS CLUB — DAY

Betty enters the officers club. She sees her father already seated at a table, across the room. He stands as she arrives at the table.

BETTY ROSS
Hi, Dad.

ROSS
Betty.

Later:

They study their menus. A waiter comes with bread and butter.

ROSS (CONT'D)
All right. I'll get right to it.

BETTY ROSS
This is about Glenn, isn't it? He's been snooping around my lab.

ROSS

Glenn noticed some things. He asked me to make some inquiries—

BETTY ROSS

—You've been spying on me. Of course.

ROSS

—Betty, listen. We've turned up some surprising things. This Krenzler you work with—You know who he really is? How much do you actually know about him?

BETTY ROSS

I think the question is: What is it that you know about him?

ROSS

Well, right now, I'm not at liberty to —

BETTY ROSS

—Not at liberty to disclose that to me. Right. You know, I was really hoping— hoping this time that you'd honestly wanted to see me again, to—(pushing her chair back) Why do I bother?—

ROSS

—You've got this all wrong, Betty.

BETTY ROSS

Do I?

ROSS

Yes. I did want to see you. I'm genuinely concerned for you.

She gets up to leave just as the waiter returns to take their order.

BETTY ROSS

I wish I could believe you.

INT. LAWRENCE BERKELEY LAB — BANNER'S LAB — NIGHT

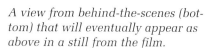

A view from behind-the-scenes (bottom) that will eventually appear as above in a still from the film.

Night: Banner still at work.

Headache. Flashes of pain.

As he works, we hear bits of his inner voice.

The phone rings. He doesn't notice. The machine picks up—we hear Betty's voice as Banner, distractedly, hears. As we listen, we see close-up the various items in the lab as Banner's eyes dart from object to object, increasingly paranoid.

> BETTY ROSS (V.O.)
> Bruce. You there?...I saw my father.... It's like he suspects you of something. Oh, I don't know. I was so impatient, as always, I should have heard him out. I just think they're planning something, with the lab, with you. Just call me, OK?

Banner's eyes. Dilation. He jumps up to get to the phone just as we hear her hang up.

He knocks over the vial of blood. It breaks, the red liquid spilling on the floor.

ABOUT ROSS

Ang's angle here is that there is something of the Hulk in all of us, this black/white thing within our character that carries the potential for disaster if we lose control. Ang talked to me at one point about the struggle within the Hulk being very much the same struggle that's within General Ross because he is as frustrated as the Hulk, or as Banner is by his situation. Ross is a powerful man, a four-star General, running this desert base but now he sees his power and his control slipping away because these private contractors are doing military work. He's losing control and therein lies his frustration; that, and the fact that Betty is involved with Bruce Banner. On some level he feels responsible for Banner because of his history with Banner's father.

Even though General Ross is a successful military career man, he has failed as a father. We can only speculate on what happened to Mrs. Ross, but I operated on the assumption that she died during childbirth and her daughter ended up looking just like her, which added another level for me in terms of how I related to my daughter.

I don't think that on a scientific level Ross has a clue what has gone on to lead to the Hulk. He knows enough of the history and sees the potential threat to his daughter to realize that it is something he must try to control. Therein lies the problem—as a military man, his instinct is to contain what he perceives to be a menace, as he has tried to do for years, which, of course, is impossible. There are a lot of sources of frustration for Ross and he is unaccustomed to that predicament, those feelings.

Sam Elliott, Actor

He looks down, horrified, frozen.

Pounding heartbeat: Title:

WHAT

AM

I?

A sound in the hallway—the dogs? He runs out.

INT. LAWRENCE BERKELEY LAB — HALLWAY — NIGHT

No one. He starts to run through the deserted halls.

Around corners, looking, searching.

Bumps into equipment cart. Pain.

Keeps running, trips, hits wall, bloody lip.

He lifts himself up, an animal cry emerging from within him.

The scream, echoing in the halls.

Now, we hear more than we see — the furious destruction of everything in arm's reach. Animal fury.

A few glimpses, reflections: huge green limbs, fists, muscles tightened.

A wall punched through.

The gammasphere thrown through the roof.

EXT. LAWRENCE BERKELEY LAB — CONTINUOUS

It lands, outside, atop a security cruiser.

Back inside:

Storyboards for the film, drawn by Mauro Borelli, were meant to look like comic book art, a style that was also used in the editing of the film. "Ang wanted comic book framing to be part of the design," says production designer Rick Heinrichs. Even though these storyboards were created very early in production, the final scene depicted in the movie hits many of the key elements shown in these drawings. Following page: For obvious reasons, the ILM artists describe this scene of the Hulk tossing the gammasphere as his "Atlas pose."

CRASH

OBLITERATION

"Whatever the Hulk came in contact with, pushed, shoved, broke, touched, or lifted was the responsibility of the physical effects crew," notes Michael Lantieri, special effects supervisor. "Ang wanted everything to be grounded in realism, so we couldn't use breakaway materials because they were too light and didn't convey the sense that something as huge and as formidable as the Hulk was there. So, when the Hulk goes on a rampage through the lab and throws a freezer against a wall and basically smashes up the place, it was all real glass or plexiglass, wood, and brick,"

This technique added another layer of challenge to an already complicated production. For one elaborate scene, Lantieri invented a giant water tank in which Eric Bana spent about two days as the imprisoned and submerged Bruce Banner; the sequence culminates when the Hulk, finally fed up, bursts through the container. Lantieri had to invent a rig so that Bana could breathe underwater and the camera crew could get the necessary shots—but the tank also had to explode, sending water cascading through the set. Lantieri's team and the construction department also had to consider the physics of capturing and directing all of the water to protect the film crew and the electrical equipment. Finally, he had to work closely with Dennis Muren and ILM, as they would have to insert the furious Hulk and possibly some CG water during post-production.

In general, to impart the Hulk's overwhelming obliteration of everything in his path, Lantieri devised elaborate mechanisms—essentially huge wire and pulley systems linking the objects of the Hulk's destructive fury to an immense source of power, generally hidden behind or below the sets, which could be destroyed or ripped down on cue. Unfortunately, these types of shots could only be filmed once and Lee set up multiple cameras to capture every angle. For one scene where the creature crashes through a laboratory and tosses a freezer through a wall, Lantieri fastened a labyrinth of steel cables to hydraulic cylinders that exerted 800 pounds of pressure and 240 pounds of pull. Rigging the equipment and positioning seven cameras took about four hours and the shot was over in less than a minute. Needless to say, so was the set.

Smash cut: the glowing eyes, alert, stopping.

Red alarm lights flash, but silently.

At the far end of the lab, the eyes detect: The Father, standing, watching.

Jump—the figure leaps and lands in front of The Father, who, oddly, shows no fear.

Silence. The Father reaches out, tenderly, with his hand, touching the green flesh.

The eyes—of the Hulk.

Calm for a moment, then filled again with fury.

Sirens in the background, coming closer.

Another scream, The Father steps back, afraid now, falling to the floor.

The sound of people yelling in the background, approaching.

Jump—the figure leaps and smashes through the roof.

EXT. LAWRENCE BERKELEY LAB — NIGHT

As the emergency vehicles arrive, the shadow of the figure merges into the trees of the Berkeley hillside.

BOUNCED

On this film, we did more wirework than anything else. We had stunts involving the trolley in San Francisco and some underwater work but the majority of our stunts involved the wires, which of course are removed in post-production.

The dogfight is primarily computer-generated. Real dogs are just not as aggressive as Hulk-dogs. Prior to the fight actually starting, the Hulk is talking to Jennifer Connelly's character and he picks her up and puts her on the roof of the car. When he sees the dogs, he takes her off the roof, puts her inside the car, and slams the door. We had to work closely with the animators on this sequence in coordinating how Jennifer gets bounced around in her harness. We had to factor in the position of his arm around her. Also, she has to bounce up and down but in the same stride as the Hulk.

Charlie Croughwell,
Stunt Coordinator

The Hulk gently lifts Betty up, places her on top of her car, so they can see eye to eye.

Then, suddenly, his eyes fill with terror.

He sniffs the air, then swiftly places his hand over her mouth, and she struggles, afraid, an image reminiscent of her earlier dream. He looks around wildly, picks her up. Her muffled cries stop.

Now silence, just the sound of the wind, Hulk crouching, listening, Betty wide-eyed, staring.

Smash cut: POV, swift movement through the forest, the sound of breathing, of powerful legs pounding on the forest floor, branches breaking.

Back to Hulk and Betty. Quiet.

POV: moving in arcs, from forest ground nearly to treetops.

Crash: The Hulk-dogs, three of them, break through the tree line, leaping right for Hulk and Betty.

Hulk leaps to the other side of Betty's car. The Hulk-dogs overshoot.

Hulk opens the car door, swiftly places Betty inside, shuts it. He rises up, to face:

The three creatures, crouching, snarling, ready to jump.

Hulk crouches again, and in an instant, leaps high into the sky, over the treetops, out of sight.

Jennifer Connelly was harnessed and lifted by wires during the filming to create the illusion that the Hulk was carrying her to safety. Below: *Original drawing by Brian O'Connell suggests the dynamic poses the Hulk might hit in the dogfight scene.*

GOING TO THE DOGS

Our last big hurdle on the show was creating the dogs. We wanted to get distinct personalities out of each dog. Smokey the mastiff is like a bear and very thick in the way he moves. He is the wrestler of the trio. Lilly the poodle is the leader and she's kind of fidgety and hyperactive. Sammy the pit bull is more like a lion; he is all about biting.

We left no stone unturned in order to deliver realistic dog performances. Even though these are Hulk-dogs, they can't simply be computer monsters, they have to move like real dogs. So we studied all kinds of dog footage from dogs in the wild to the pets brought to work by our crew. Re-creating the sloppiness of foot slips was essential to remove the computer-generated look. We even motion-captured attack dogs attacking a person in a bite suit. We created libraries of motion-captured runs, leaps, and bites. Some of this motion could be directly mapped onto the Hulk-dogs, but usually the mo-cap was edited. In the end, I would say that the dogs were 50 percent mo-cap and 50 percent hand-animated.

Colin Brady,
Animation Director

Inset above: *Drawing by Jim Carson with the Hulk maquette is meant to show the scale comparison of the Hulk and the three Hulk-dogs.* Right: *Alex Jaeger concept painting of the Hulk poodle used as a guide for CG fur development, particularly to maintain a matted, disheveled quality. Sculpted maquette and real photo were used as reference.* Far right: *Storyboard art by Michael Jackson.*

The dogs, confused, circle themselves, leap, but not high enough, fall.

They regroup. Then, Hulk descends, landing on Hulk-dog #1's back. Snap! The animal lets out a hideous, dying yelp, as Hulk bounces back up into the air and away.

As the Hulk-dog expires, its flesh begins to steam and melt away.

Betty's POV from the car. Hulk-dogs #2 and #3 circle even more wildly.

Hulk descends again, but this time misses his target. Now the real fight begins.

Now dog #2 clamps onto Hulk's ankle. Hulk lets out a roar, as dog #3 recovers, leaps straight for his neck.

Hulk hears Betty's screams, but is blocked by dog #2, who menacingly advances on him. He jumps atop the cabin, then to a treetop.

The creatures sneer; Hulk is seemingly vanquished, afraid.

Betty: terrified, she screams.

The dogs hear her, turn, and circle the car.

DOGFIGHT

In one sequence Hulk meets and fights three dogs that Bruce's dad has created as part of his experiments. They're sort of half Hulk-dogs, six feet tall and ten feet long. There are three different breeds and they've been trained to go after Betty's scent. They're trying to get her, but Hulk is there, thank God, at the right moment to protect her from them. The Hulk has quite a difficult fight with the dogs; the scene takes place at nighttime in the mountains at her cabin retreat. These are ferocious dogs and the Hulk's a big guy so the sequence is quite exciting. We didn't want to be too vicious about it—these are pretend dogs—but we had fun with the scene.

Dennis Muren,
Visual Effects Supervisor

Cinematographer Fred Elmes shoots a close-up of the animatronic version of the Hulk poodle. The puppet head was only used in a few brief cutaways as the Hulk-dogs were created by computer graphics.

A huge paw on the windshield. Fangs. Another paw, this time harder. The windshield begins to crack.

Then, a shadow falls over the windshield. In a blur, Hulk brings down an enormous redwood tree that he has uprooted, squashing #2, whose face smashes partially through the windshield, inches from Betty.

Meanwhile, the last dog and Hulk are locked in a deadly embrace, rolling, biting, mauling, choking.

Betty stares horrified into the dying light of dog #2's eyes, as she tries to pull herself back. Suddenly the dog's eyes pop open with one last burst of energy. His jaws widen, his fangs lift and smash through the glass, but his mouth only partially closes around Betty, as he finally expires, and begins to melt.

Dog #3 gets his fangs around Hulk's neck. Hulk freezes, tenses, drops his arms. As the dog tries to work his teeth into the Hulk, we see Hulk's neck muscles ripple, condense, and start to grow—they push out against the dog's teeth. We feel the dog begin to sense the outcome; we hear the beginnings of a whimper, as Hulk stares down into his face, and then, with one hand, grabs the dog's skull and squeezes the life out of him. The creature's body steamily melts away.

Dawn approaches, a faint light beginning to fill the sky, reflecting lightly of the surface of the lake.

Hulk stumbles to the water's edge.

He looks down, confused, fearful of his own image reflecting back at him in the water.

The image starts to break up.

Hulk looks to the sky: clouds, a light rain beginning to fall, mottling Hulk's image in the water...

He raises his face to the sky, closes his eyes.

And then, as if in a dream, Hulk begins to transform, back to Banner, as if the rain were washing him, back to himself.

Betty's POV, from behind the smashed glass, the rain drops, she can barely see what's happening as the figure sinks to the ground.

Then, Banner rises. Sees her.

He walks to the car, struggles and finally pulls open the crushed door, and takes the bloodied Betty into his arms.

They lie down huddled together. Banner, naked, now cradled in her arms.

They look into each other's faces. Banner lets out a cry.

Then: He holds out his hand in front of him, makes a fist, punches the air in front of him, close to Betty's face. She winces. He laughs, almost manically.

> BRUCE BANNER
> He sent his dogs, but I killed them, right?
> I killed them!

He grabs her—comes back to his senses. A look of fear in his eyes. He shakes his head. He looks again at his hand, his fist. She takes it gently in her hands. She holds him.

INT. BETTY'S CABIN — NIGHT/EXT

It's a few minutes later as she wraps a blanket around his trembling form.

> BETTY ROSS
> (keyed up)
> Bruce, you have to help me. I don't under-
> stand what I just saw.

> BRUCE BANNER
> I got mad...and then...

> BETTY ROSS
> It must be the nanomeds. It must be the
> gamma exposure. But we've never seen
> any effect like this before.

RAGE

POWER

FREEDOM

> BRUCE BANNER
> No. Deeper. The gammas just...unleashed whatever was already there.

> BETTY ROSS
> Unleashed what?

> BRUCE BANNER
> (unsure)
> Me. It.
> (getting upset)
> I don't...

> BETTY ROSS
> It's OK, it's OK....what were those animals?

> BRUCE BANNER
> My father sent them....He is my father.

He thinks about that a moment, overwhelmed. Looks back at her.

> BRUCE BANNER (CONT'D)
> He wanted me to change. He wanted me to change into that mindless...
> Hulk....Why would he want that?

> BETTY ROSS
> Can you remember anything? Is there anything from when you were changed?

> BRUCE BANNER
> It's like a dream.

> BETTY ROSS
> About what?

> BRUCE BANNER
> Rage. Power.
> (searches)
> Freedom.
> (smiles wearily)

He is already drifting off. She holds him, thinking.

INT. REDWOOD CABIN — KITCHEN — DAY

Betty tiptoes into the kitchen, away from Banner.

She picks up the phone, dials a number.

Intercut:

INT. JOINT TACTICAL FORCE WEST — MAIN HALLWAY — DAY

An aide hands Ross a mobile phone as Ross strides across the hallway.

> BETTY ROSS (V.O.)
> (whispering into the phone)
> Dad.

ROSS
Betty! Are you all right?

BETTY ROSS
—I'm scared, I need your help.

ROSS
Where are you?

BETTY ROSS
I need to trust you.

Bruce stirs slightly—she pauses, watches him.

ROSS
Yes? Betty? Betty?

EXT. REDWOOD CABIN — DAY

To establish. The wind. Quiet.

INT. REDWOOD CABIN — DAY

BETTY ROSS
How are you feeling?

BRUCE BANNER
OK, I guess.

BETTY ROSS
I think that somehow the anger you felt
last night is triggering the nanomeds.

BRUCE BANNER
How could it? We designed them to
respond to physical damage.

BETTY ROSS
Emotional damage can manifest physically.

BRUCE BANNER
Like what?

BETTY ROSS
A serious trauma…a suppressed memory.

BRUCE BANNER
Your father grilled me about something I
was suppose to remember from early
childhood.

BETTY ROSS
He did?

BRUCE BANNER
Yeah. It sounded bad. But I just honestly
don't remember.

BETTY ROSS
What worries me is that a physical wound
is finite, but with emotions, what's to stop
it from going on and on, and starting a
chain reaction?

*Body proportions guide, by visual
effects art director Wilson Tang.*

IT'S THE HULK

Motion-capture has its bene-
fits, but we didn't want to start
with it because although it provides the computer with a sense
of the way a body moves in
space, it still can be a bit re-
stricting. People tend to freeze
up when they do it. It's always
awkward to be in that suit with
these electrodes stuck to you
with a bunch of people around
watching…plus there is a typically
a time or budget constraint. Ang
didn't want the Hulk to be too
lumbering or muscle-bound. Be-
sides, ultimately, why would we
want to be limited to just what a
human can do? It's the Hulk.

Colin Brady,
Animation Director

> **BRUCE BANNER**
> Maybe next time, it'll just keep going. You know what scares me the most though? When it happens, when it comes over me—when I totally lose control—

They lock glances.

> **BRUCE BANNER (CONT'D)**
> I like it.

A moment of silence.

A noise outside. Banner goes to the window to see what it was.

> A popping sound—a tranquilizer dart hits Banner in the leg. He sinks to the ground.

> **BRUCE BANNER (CONT'D)**
> What?

Betty goes to him, helps him to the ground.

> **BETTY ROSS**
> It's going to be all right. I'm sorry. It's just going to make you sleep. I'm going to take you some place safe.

The door bursts open: gas-masked tactical team, weapons drawn, enters.

EXT. SKY CRANE HELICOPTER — DAY

The giant helicopter, escorted by a pair of fighter choppers, high above the clouds.

EXT. DESERT BASE — DAY

The sky crane unloads a large container onto a transport truck.

EXT. CONVOY — DAY

A convoy pulls up behind the tattered screen of an old drive-in movie theater.

INT. DESERT BASE — UNDERGROUND LOADING DOCK — DAY

The convoy stops. From the back of a truck, troops unload the tube.

INT. DESERT BASE — TUNNEL — CONTINUOUS

The tube moves along the track, down the tunnel—deep underground into the mountain.

INT. DESERT BASE — MAIN HALL — CONTINUOUS

The tube is unloaded into the vast underground arrival hall, filled with military personnel, scientists, technicians, moving in and out of various tunnels that radiate outward from this main hub. A command and control center is perched high above the hall, with windows overlooking it.

INT. DESERT BASE — CONTAINMENT CELL — DAY

Banner, still in a drug-induced sleep, inside a spherical containment cell.

INT. DESERT BASE — ROSS'S OFFICE — DAY

Betty and Dad are in it already, tempers high.

> BETTY ROSS
> We're buried out here in the middle of nowhere. How long are you going to keep Bruce sedated?

Top: The walls and floor of the convoy scene were created as a matte painting by Jules Mann. Below: Three storyboards by Jim Martin illustrate the underground lab where the Hulk is taken prisoner.

DESERT BASE

Production designer Rick Heinrichs followed Ang Lee's dictate for reality, but with a certain amount of leeway, specifically with regard to the subterranean government base where the captured Hulk is taken.

Given the secret nature of such bases, not a great deal of information was available, although Heinrichs did study some photos of NORAD—which he used as a basis for his imaginative design of rabbit warren-like, interconnected series of hallways, claustrophobic tunnels, and dehumanizing labs and offices. Heinrichs used bright colors in this set—yellows, greens, oranges, and reds—and against the industrial grays of the tunnels, the appearance was, well, almost comic book.

"The truth is the government uses those colors in buildings. They all mean something. We just pushed them a little bit," Heinrichs says.

Below: *Art by Jim Martin visualizing ideas for the underground lab.*

Top: *Art by Jim Martin of the underground lab.* Below left: *Director Ang Lee and producer Larry Franco discuss the set model for the desert base building.* Below right: *The top image is an early concept model for the underground lab and the bottom image is the actual set as it was filmed.*

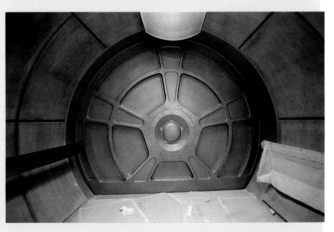

ROSS

The rest of his natural life, if I have to.

BETTY ROSS

You said I could trust you.

ROSS

I'm your father. You can trust me to do what I think is right, not what you think you want.

BETTY ROSS

He's a human being.

ROSS

He's also something else. Suppose he gets out—has one of his mood swings in a populated area?

BETTY ROSS

I'm aware of the potential danger. I'm also aware that he saved my life.

ROSS

Yeah, from a mutant French poodle. Betty, I've got three men in the hospital, Talbot barely walking—what do you want me to do?

BETTY ROSS

I want you to help him. Why isn't that simple? Why is he such a threat to you?

ROSS

Because I know what he comes from! He's his father's son, every last molecule of him. He says he doesn't know his father— he's working in the exact same goddamn field his father did. So either he's lying, or it's far worse than that, and he's…

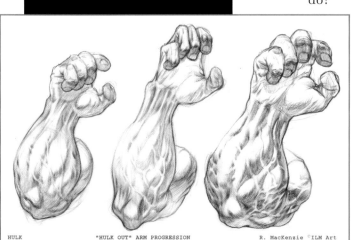

Detail drawing by Brian O'Connell showing the arm of Bruce Banner hulking out.

BETTY ROSS

What? Predestined? To follow in his father's footsteps?

ROSS

I was gonna say "damned."

96

> BETTY ROSS
> Of course you were. But I'm a scientist,
> Dad. I believe this can be figured out.
> That Bruce can be helped.

> ROSS
> I know you do. Whether you know or
> care, I have a lot of pride in what you've
> done. I just can't shake the feeling that
> we're all...

> BETTY ROSS
> Damned?

> ROSS
> We shouldn't be here, Betty. Back here of
> all places. Too many floatin' damn ghosts.
> I feel like this is exactly what David
> Banner wanted.

She comes around, having none of his fatalistic reverie.

> BETTY ROSS
> Look, I know the government thinks they
> have a weapon on their hands or he'd be
> dead already. They can probe and prod all
> they want, but in the meanwhile, you
> have to let me help him. Nobody knows
> him better than I do.

A beat, he sizes up her offer.

> BETTY ROSS (CONT'D)
> What did David Banner do to him?

EXT. FATHER'S HOUSE — DAY

An FBI tactical team surrounds the house.

INT. FATHER'S HOUSE —
CONTINUOUS

They burst down the door. The place is a
deserted wreck.

INT. LAWRENCE BERKELEY LAB —
HALLWAY — NIGHT

The wheels of the janitor's cart. Moving
slowly down a hall.

The door to the gammasphere is opened.

INT. LAWRENCE BERKELEY LAB —
GAMMASPHERE — NIGHT

The place is still pretty much a shambles.

Swiftly, hands rig up a series of makeshift reflectors
around the edge of the vacuum tubes protruding into the
room.

ALS

While Telegraph Hill was
not new to moviemaking, *The
Hulk* did break new ground at
Berkeley, becoming the first
production to film the
renowned Advanced Light
Source (ALS)—a sprawling,
Byzantine contraption that
generates intense light for
scientific and technological
research that is situated
near the Lab's equally famous
cyclotron. In a fitting bit of
"movie reality," its grounds
were also the spot where the
Hulk tosses the gammas-
phere onto a police car.

*Behind the scenes view of the FBI
tactical team storming the house
of the Father.*

97

FT-07
08:40:21:04:D2

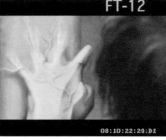

FT-12
08:10:22:28:D2

FT-10
09:45:51:21:B2

FT-13
09:50:06:09:D2

FT-11
10:07:57:20:A2

FT-14
08:41:07:29:C2

CUT TO:

Later, The Father stands in the middle of the wrecked gammasphere, his arms out-stretched, the chamber filled with light and radiation, an open canister emitting gas at his feet.

A blissful smile transforms his face.

The gammasphere shuts down. Light returns to normal. He drops to his knees.

FATHER
Yes.

He grabs the edge of a table to help him stand, looks down at his hand: It's been cut slightly from the edge of the metallic table, a tiny rip, a thin strip of blood.

He takes a handkerchief, holds it to his hand. We see the tissue around the cut begin to take on the characteristics of the cotton cloth.

The Father frowns, takes the kerchief away, looks at his hand, thinks, then presses it to the table.

His hand and wrist take on a metallic glow. He pulls his hand away, studies it again, then turns quickly and slams his hand into the wall, easily smashing through it.

He laughs.

Just then, the door opens. A security guard pokes his head in.

GUARD
What's happening here?

FATHER
Look. My hand. You see, the strength of my son's DNA, combined with the radiant energy, it's transformed my cells, allowing them, after exposure to other cellular structures, to absorb and replicate them—

The guard slowly goes for his gun.

GUARD
I'm gonna have to ask you to put your hands up, pal. OK? Nice and easy.

The guard approaches The Father, who starts again to laugh.

He brings his metallic hand down on the guard's head, a sickening metallic thud. The guard goes down.

The Father smiles, wiggles his metallic fingers.

INT. DESERT BASE — CONTAINMENT CELL — DAY

Betty smooths her hand through Banner's hair, as he wakes up.

> BRUCE BANNER
> Where am I?

> BETTY ROSS
> You're home.

EXT. DESERT BASE — COMMERCIAL DISTRICT — DAY

Betty and Banner walk through the deserted ramshackle street. At a not-too-discreet distance, troops armed with various hi-tech containment weapons and lightweight attack vehicles moving slowly behind them.

> BETTY ROSS
> It's hard to believe we used to live here.

They keep walking.

> BRUCE BANNER
> I must have seen you or known you. If only I could remember.

Betty has no response.

Banner walks a few steps away, falls into a reverie.

The wind. Dust.

EXT. DESERT BASE — ABANDONED NEIGHBORHOOD — DAY

They wander among the broken-down, deserted houses.

An abandoned swingset. Betty sits on it, absentmindedly swings.

On Banner: the sound of the rusty swing.

Banner notices a particular house nearby. Banner pauses, senses it might have been his.

He walks toward the house.

Betty gets off the swing, follows.

EXT./INT. DESERT BASE — OLD HOUSE — DAY

Bruce and Betty wander through the deserted backyard area, moving slowly toward the house.

> BRUCE BANNER
> It's my old house, isn't it?

The door opens, but no one enters. Dust...sunlight...After a beat, Bruce walks through with Betty a half step behind him.

Bruce walks into the center of the room. Looks around. The place is empty—dusty relics. NO furniture. Just architecture.

> BRUCE BANNER (CONT'D)
> (turns to the door)
> Let's go.

> BETTY ROSS
> (stops him)
> Please try.

CLOSER.

They stand face to face. Bruce moves back deeper into the room. He glances to his left. Shattered window. He wanders toward a closed door leading to the back of the house.

This stops him. Banner looks at the door, then crouches.

> BETTY ROSS (CONT'D)
> What is it?

> BRUCE BANNER
> (cold)
> Nothing.

> BETTY ROSS
> (re: his comment)
> Really.

> BRUCE BANNER
> Dammit. This is just another problem that you want to solve. Well OK, Betty. What do you want to know?

> BETTY ROSS
> What was in that room?

Face to face...Betty heads toward the closed door. Bruce hurries to stop her.

> BETTY ROSS (CONT'D)
> What are you afraid I'll see?

She reaches up and touches the side of his face. An artery BULGES then recedes. His jaw juts forward.

A low guttural sound comes out. His arms have started to bulge.

> BETTY ROSS (CONT'D)
> Trust me.

Behind the scenes with director Ang Lee, atop a ladder for a better view of a shot in the desert

THE COLOR OF HULK

In the comics, the Hulk is a supersaturated green; this is what Ang wanted and it's been very, very hard for us to work with that color. It reacts differently than expected. You put a blue light on it, nothing happens; you add a red light, nothing happens; it still looks day-glow green. It's so intense that it doesn't react to lights in the usual way. When, for example, you put a blue light on an actor, the skin color changes, and he fits in with his blue-lit surroundings. Put a blue light on this green and it's still green. We had about a year of conversations and development for the color. We played with various subsurface hues and amounts, different skin saturations and intensities, an array of translucencies and surface details, until finally arriving at something that maintained Ang's vision of the Hulk and gave us a believable creature.

Creating the nighttime scenes was a little more forgiving because we could play up that it was dramatically lit along with keeping a sense of mystery. In broad daylight, the sun is blasting the character and it was incredibly challenging because every single pore, follicle, hair, and blemish showed. The Hulk is certainly one of the most complex creatures we've ever done at ILM. There are a lot of characters out there in recent movies that have flesh tone and I initially thought it would be easier to create a green guy because it was one level removed from reality but it has proven to be much harder. We are working in the state-of-the-art at the moment but we are still always developing and changing and pushing the boundaries. It has been a very interesting journey.

Christopher Townsend,
Computer Graphics Supervisor

The sound turns into a roar. He whirls away from her and suddenly kicks down the door.

FROM THE OTHER SIDE.

An explosion of light and dust. When it clears, Banner is standing there again... perfectly composed. Perfectly restored. The storm has passed—the impulse is gone.

REVERSE ANGLE — THEIR POV

The room is empty. Just a shell. There's nothing there.

> BRUCE BANNER
> (turns)
> See. There's nothing.
> (re: himself?)
> It's empty.

ANGLE. BETTY.

It's devastating. He looks her in the eye: collected...cold...dispassionate...composed. She steadies herself on a door. It's empty.

INT. DESERT BASE — HALLWAY — ROSS'S OFFICE — DAY

Betty places her thumb on a biometric reader at the door to the control room. The door remains locked.

She tries it again. Red light on the lock.

INT. DESERT BASE — ROSS'S OFFICE — DAY

Later, inside Ross's office:

> ROSS
> They have explicitly
> limited my jurisdiction
> and your access has
> been denied. NSA has
> decided to hand over the
> study of the—the
> threat—to Atheon.

> BETTY ROSS
> But you're the head of
> this base, you're in
> charge.

> ROSS
> But I don't set policy
> and I still take orders

For a brief moment, he loses his cool.

>   ROSS
>   (CONT'D)
> I can't believe Talbot would go around me like this. There are a lot of powerful peo-ple interested in what's going on here, and money to be made, lots of it. You know the worst part about all this?

He slumps in his chair. She thinks about going to him, but holds back.

He gives her a nod of appreciation.

>   ROSS
> When I had Banner locked up and sent the boy off, I didn't give the kid a second thought. He was just collateral damage. Well, he isn't anymore, is he?

>   BETTY ROSS
> So what can I do?

>   ROSS
> You can go home. I'd tell you to go and

Above left: *Ang Lee examines a life-size sculpture of the Hulk caught in foam that was used during the sequence where he escapes from the water tank.* Below: *Facial and upper body correctives for the Hulk drawn by visual effects art director Wilson Tang.*

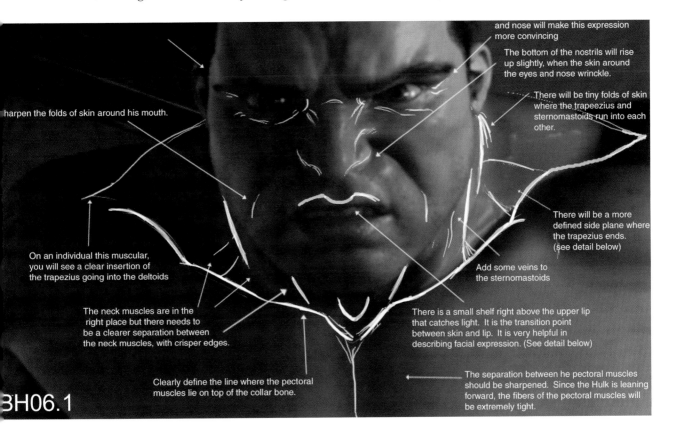

harpen the folds of skin around his mouth.

and nose will make this expression more convincing

The bottom of the nostrils will rise up slightly, when the skin around the eyes and nose wrinkle.

There will be tiny folds of skin where the trapeezius and sternomastoids run into each other.

There will be a more defined side plane where the trapezius ends. (see detail below)

On an individual this muscular, you will see a clear insertion of the trapezius going into the deltoids

Add some veins to the sternomastoids

The neck muscles are in the right place but there needs to be a clearer separation between the neck muscles, with crisper edges.

There is a small shelf right above the upper lip that catches light. It is the transition point between skin and lip. It is very helpful in describing facial expression. (See detail below)

Clearly define the line where the pectoral muscles lie on top of the collar bone.

The separation between he pectoral muscles should be sharpened. Since the Hulk is leaning forward, the fibers of the pectoral muscles will be extremely tight.

BH06.1

say goodbye to him, but I've been informed that for now all further contact is out of the question.

It starts to sink in.

I/E. HELICOPTER — DAY

Betty looks down from her seat in the chopper at the desolate desert floor as she flies home.

INT. DESERT BASE — CONTAINMENT CELL — DAY

A number of small openings in the walls mechanically appear; gun barrels, red laser aim dots appear all over Banner.

The door bursts open, startling Banner

Talbot sweeps in, carrying what looks like an electrified walking stick. He's still a bit bruised from his last encounter with Banner.

> TALBOT
> Hiya, Bruce. How you feeling? Grub OK here for you?

> BRUCE BANNER
> You're looking a little worse for wear.

> TALBOT
> I'm fine and dandy. Might need a little reconstructive work on my left index finger. Insurance'll cover it.

> BRUCE BANNER
> What are you doing here?

> TALBOT
> Good question. See, I need your cells to trigger some chemical distress signals....You know, so you can get a little green for me again, and then I'll carve off a piece of the real you, analyze it, patent it, make a fortune. You mind?

> BRUCE BANNER
> I'll never let you.

> TALBOT
> I'm not sure you have much of a choice.

With this, Talbot takes his stick and smashes it against Banner's stomach. It's an electric stun gun, and Banner goes flying backwards against the wall.

TALBOT (CONT'D)

C'mon Bruce, aren't you feeling a little angry? After all, you have only me to play with, now that Betty's dumped you and gone back to Berkeley.

BRUCE BANNER

You're lying.

TALBOT

You know, for me this is a win-win situation. You turn green, all these guys kill you, and I perform the autopsy. You don't, I mop the floor with you, and (whispering) maybe by accident I go too far and break your neck. (beat) Bad science maybe, but personally gratifying. Come to think of it, you are looking a little green—around the gills.

Banner, using the wall for support, gets back up. He continues to stare at him—but still no Hulk.

TALBOT (CONT'D)

C'mon. Just a love tap. Let's see what you've got.

BRUCE BANNER
(weakly)
Never.

Banner stumbles towards him. Talbot, not as scared as before, drops the stick and pummels him with his fists, finally planting a right hook on his chin, knocking him out.

He moves over to Banner's crumpled body, kicks it.

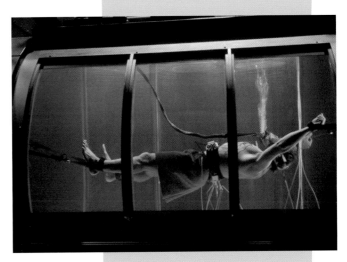

TALBOT

You know, consciously you might control it. But subconsciously, I bet that's another story.

INT. DESERT BASE — IMMERSION CELL — DAY

Banner, unconscious, floats in an immersion tank, wired to various instruments.

INT. DESERT BASE — ATHEON IMMERSION LAB — DAY

Talbot, watching on the monitors, going over the read-outs.

TALBOT

Let's jump-start those brain waves, shall we?

Back on Banner: slight twitching.

Above: *Production illustration of Bruce Banner floating in the water tank by Rodolfo Damaggio.* Below: *A still from the location shoot of Eric Bana floating in the tank. This image was used by the ILM artists to create the escape scene for the Hulk.*

THE PURPLE SHORTS

At some point in the course of the movie, Bruce Banner had to wear the trademark purple shorts made popular in the original comic book. This garb proved to be tricky. Costume designer Marit Allen had to compensate for the Hulk's huge growth spurt. Logically, she says, the Banner/Hulk transformation would rip puny human clothing to shreds. Indeed at a certain point in the film, the Hulk stomps about completely naked and Banner is likewise exposed in his post-Hulk position. However, Allen decided the violet pants would be a jersey material that stretched, to some extent, and tore as the Hulk expanded, but didn't disintegrate.

EXT. BETTY'S HOUSE — DAY

A van pulls up, Betty gets out and goes inside. The van remains parked outside of the house.

INT. BETTY'S HOUSE — DAY

Betty enters, senses something is wrong: In a chair, the Father sits, waiting for her.

> FATHER
> (rising)
> My dear Miss Ross, welcome back.

> BETTY ROSS
> (backing toward the door)
> Look, there are two MPs right outside.

> FATHER
> —You don't have to worry. I'm not angry with you, not anymore. Please…

> BETTY ROSS
> What do you want?

> FATHER
> It's over for me now, I know that—and it'll soon be over for him. That's why I've come to you—to ask you, Miss Ross, if you think you can persuade your father— as a man—as a father himself—if I turn myself in peacefully…then he can put me away forever…to let me see my son one last time. Could you do that for me?

> BETTY ROSS
> (softening)
> It's out of my father's hands now.

> FATHER
> I understand…they turned him into a puppet. I can't blame him.

> BETTY ROSS
> You shouldn't. You should blame yourself for what you've done to your son.

> FATHER
> And what did I do to him, Miss Ross? Nothing! I tried to overcome the limits in myself—myself, not him. Can you understand? To improve on nature, my nature. Knowledge of oneself, that is the only path to the truth that gives men the power to defy God's boundaries (and operate beyond prejudice).

> BETTY ROSS
> You wanna know what's beyond your boundaries? Other people. Connecting with others makes you greater than you

were, but you never will, and neither can Bruce. All he knows is fear, fear of life.

From The Father, resignation, a sigh.

> FATHER
> Fear? Perhaps Miss Ross, and loneliness, too? Yes, I've felt them both. But I have lived, lived completely, once…a taste of another, in her reality…her presence.

Betty listens as he seems to drift into a reverie. He smiles to himself.

> FATHER (CONT'D)
> You see, I was so in love with her…And she so wanted a child, my child.

INTERCUT:

INT. DESERT BASE — IMMERSION CELL — DAY

On Banner.

The wires.

Entering his brain.

We see a vast neural network, reticulated nets, forming floating, liquid screens of unconscious images, memories. We hear the uncharted chorus of voices and sounds inside him, sometimes blending with his father's voice as he tells Betty their story.

INT. DESERT BASE — ATHEON LAB — CONTINUOUS

Talbot and team work on.

> FATHER (V.O.)
> I could feel it, from the moment she conceived—it wasn't a son I had given her, but something else, a monster maybe, something inexplicable. I should have put a stop to it right then, but I was curious— that was my downfall. And as I watched his tiny life unfold—and I began to imagine the horror of it—my curiosity was replaced by compassion.

INT. DESERT BASE — IMMERSION CELL — CONTINUOUS

Inside Banner's unconscious, the images start to connect, take shape.

The dolls.

Young Banner, playing.

His mother, smiling.

His mother takes him in her arms.

Smiling, reassuring.

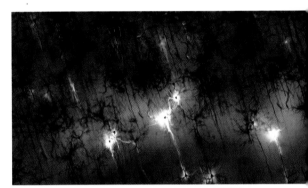
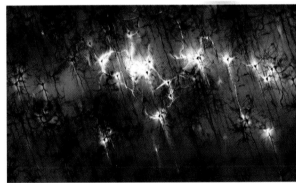

Concept art by Gus Dizon of what the Hulk's neurons look like when he gets angry. The idea of these concept paintings was to create the life and death of the cell in a painterly way. According to Wilson Tang, the ILM artists were greatly influenced by the work of Jackson Pollock.

107

The door opens. Anxious now, she turns.

> FATHER (V.O.)
> But then, they took away my chance to
> cure him, your father threw me out and I
> had nothing left to give him. I remember
> that day so well, every sensation, walking
> into the house. Feeling the handle of the
> knife in my hand. I knew I was doing a
> father's work, fulfilling a father's mercy.

INT. DESERT BASE — IMMERSION CELL —
CONTINUOUS

Banner's eyelids—beneath, the eyes spinning.

More memories:

A glimpse of David Banner.

Bruce's mother goes to him in the other room.

The toys.

Arguing.

A scream. She's been stabbed.

A knife, bloody, drops to the floor.

> FATHER (V.O.)
> But she surprised me. It was as if she
> and the knife merged. You can't imag-
> ine—the unbearable finality of it—
> her life, and mine, suspended at the
> end of my hand.

Young Bruce takes the knife, flies at his father.

Mother, stumbling into the desert.

> FATHER (CONT'D)
> And in that one moment, I took every
> thing that was dear to me and trans-
> formed it into nothing more than a
> memory.

MPs swarm the house.

His father, put in an ambulance.

Young Bruce crying, pointing to the desert, as
they drag him away.

The sun. The desert.

An empty swing on the playground, rocking back and
forth.

Back to the immersion tank: Banner's face.

INT. BETTY'S HOUSE — CONTINUOUS

FATHER
You see, Miss Ross, you can't step back from what you create. You must learn, simply, to embrace it, to love it, as I love him.

He starts to weep.

Betty regards him uneasily.

BETTY ROSS
Let me make a call.

She leaves the room.

He looks after her: a grim smile replacing his tears.

The camera punches in on his grinning mouth.

INT. DESERT BASE — IMMERSION CELL — CONTINUOUS

The Father's grinning mouth is replaced by the twisted mouth of Banner, in agony: a muffled, liquid scream.

Banner, his face a vision of pain, his body distending.

INT. DESERT BASE — ATHEON IMMERSION LAB — DAY

TECHNICIAN
We're getting a lot of neural activity.

The monitors flash.

TECHNICIAN (CONT'D)
Incredible. He's generating enormous amounts of—

TALBOT
Let me see. (beat) Bingo! That must be some jumbo nightmare he's having. Do it now. Start the enzyme extraction.

TECHNICIAN TWO
Sir—negative drill penetration.

TALBOT
Dammit! Stick him harder. Give me full RPMs.

INT. DESERT BASE — IMMERSION CELL — CONTINUOUS

On Banner. The pain of recognition, as his past comes to consciousness.

In the fluid environment, his body writhes, twists.

And then—Hulk out.

Below: *In their original concept art, Wilson Tang and Robert MacKenzie visualize the idea of a single thought radiating outwards within the mind of the Hulk. Following pages: The scene of the Hulk's escape from the tank is a good example of the most challenging aspect of computer graphics, which is to create anything organic, such as water or skin. In this scene, ILM artists added floods of splashing water and bulging muscles on the Hulk as he slams his way out of the glass tank.*

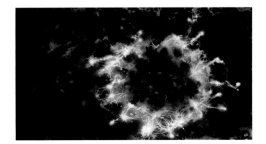

We hear the muted roar of his cries from inside the tank, creating their own waves in the liquid, resonating, finally cracking the tank.

A small flood, as Hulk stands, emerges.

Intercut:

The lab control room, as Talbot and the others react.

> TECH
> Should I incinerate?

> TALBOT
> No. I can't do anything with ashes.

Talbot hits the intercom.

> TALBOT (CONT'D)
> All right. Put him to sleep.

Back to Hulk:

He roars. Pounds against the walls of the immersion cell.

Gas flows from the walls, enveloping him; he responds not by fainting but as if it were a nasty allergen. He flails harder; a final fist gets his arm through the wall and into the hallway.

INT. DESERT BASE — ATHEON HALLWAY — CONTINUOUS

Hulk emerges into the hallway, gas flowing behind him. Various personnel are immediately overcome by the gas, as Hulk makes his way down the hall.

INT. DESERT BASE — ATHEON IMMERSION LAB — CONTINUOUS

> TALBOT
> Non-lethals only. I must get a sample of him. Hit him with the foam.

INT. DESERT BASE — ATHEON HALLWAY — CONTINUOUS

A group of Atheon security

round the corner, face Hulk at the other end of the hallway.

INT. DESERT BASE —
COMMAND AND CONTROL —
CONTINUOUS

Hulk in the hallway shows up on
the monitors in front of ROSS.

>   AIDE
>   Sir.

>   ROSS
>   Jesus. Get me Talbot.

INT. DESERT BASE — ATHEON
HALLWAY — CONTINUOUS

One of the techies steps forward
with a large barreled gun attached
to two tanks on his back and fires.
A stream of gelatinous liquid covers
Hulk in sticky foam. Hulk is stuck.
Struggling.

The liquid starts to congeal
around him.

He flicks some of it off; it lands on
one of the men who is instantly
frozen in it.

Intercut ROSS:

>   ROSS
>   Talbot, this is Ross. Talk
>   to me.

Intercut Talbot:

>   TALBOT
>   Under control, General. I'll
>   let you know if we need
>   you.

>   ROSS
>   Unacceptable. Unseat your
>   asses down there, immedi-
>   ately. I want a full-court
>   evacuation now. I'm shut-
>   ting you down.

Talbot throws down his mike.
Looks at his screen: Hulk, still
struggling against the super-goo.

>   TALBOT
>   (to the tech)
>   Lock down.

>   TECHNICIAN
>   But, didn't you just hear
>   the general?

Talbot gets up, pulls a sidearm.

> TALBOT
> I said lock down.

INT. DESERT BASE —
ATHEON HALLWAY —
CONTINUOUS

> SOLDIER
> Response force heading
> for South 4-11.

Huge metal doors descend,
closing off the Atheon lab
areas, just as ROSS's troops
attempt to enter.

> SOLDIER
> (CONT'D)
> C2 this is O4. Doors
> are down.

INT. DESERT BASE —
ATHEON HALLWAY —
CONTINUOUS

Talbot moves with a contin-
gent of Atheon security, some
of them armed.

They pause as they hear Hulk
around the corner.

> TALBOT
> Let's get a sample of
> him.

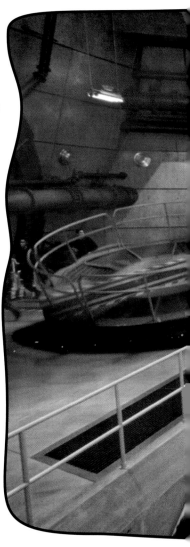

They take the corner, face Hulk, who is still mired in the foam.

Talbot cautiously approaches Hulk.

> TALBOT (CONT'D)
> Now, let's take this nice and easy.

Talbot takes a hand-held laser drill and punches it into Hulk's neck.

Hulk recoils, screaming, as, his skin tearing, he begins to free himself from the foam. Talbot steps back.

> TALBOT (CONT'D)
> Pull back.

The men retreat around a corner, Hulk following. With each footstep, he shakes the halls.

Another corner: at the far end of this hall, the metal doors are starting to rise, troops at the ready on the other side.

Talbot pauses, grabs a super-huge kick-ass automatic weapon from one of the other men, stands his ground.

Hulk and Talbot eye each other. Hulk snarls, and then, before Talbot's eyes, he grows again—this time from twelve to fifteen feet high, so big he fills the tunnel, crouching. Talbot, temporarily transfixed, afraid, watches in awe.

Troops rushing in the adjoining hall.

>   TALBOT (CONT'D)
>   So long, big boy.

Talbot sprays Hulk with a hail of powerful automatic fire. Hulk contorts in pain as the bullets make contact.

We hear: metallic pinging, as the bullets bounce off of him.

Talbot's face: registering his mistake.

The bullets bounce back, riddling Talbot, who crumples to the ground.

The troops: witnessing it all, turn tail and run for it.

INT. DESERT BASE — COMMAND CENTER — DAY — CONTINUOUS

>   ROSS
>   Lock down the entire facility
>   immediately!

116

OLIVER
Target's still moving towards blue level.

ROSS
Evacuate the main hall.

INT. DESERT BASE — MAIN HALL — CONTINUOUS

Hulk bursts through the main elevator shaft breaking the elevator base free. He nudges the base with his shoulder as he climbs out the shaft sending it rolling toward the military personnel. They scatter.

Intercut:

Ross watches as his team is overpowered by the Hulk. He realizes they are inadequate....

Intercut:

Hulk destroys the lower loading dock area and engages the heavy weapons team as they run toward him from the tunnel.

Hulk kicks a large cargo cart across the deck. The cart slams into a stack of radiological contamination barrels causing an explosion of toxic gas. An electrical panel explodes in a shower of sparks. A steam line ruptures spewing high pressure steam....The cart collides into the heavy weapons team sending the men flying like bowling pins.

Hulk steps back up on the mid-level. He sees two soldiers on the catwalk still firing their weapons. Hulk looks for something to throw at them....Turning, he hits his face against a stationary crane holding a suspended crate. Angered, Hulk grabs the crane and sends it flying down the track smashing through the windows.

Ross weighs his options. Stay and fight or release Hulk towards the open ground to better utilize his assets.

Intercut:

Back on the upper level...

Hulk grabs the discarded elevator base and looks towards the command and control center windows.

Intercut:
Everyone's face as they realize...

> ROSS
> Incoming!

Everyone scrambles and hits the floor taking cover as Hulk throws the base through the window. The base flies across the room and imbeds into a wall of video monitors.

The power flickers...sparks fly...

> ROSS
> Shut down all power to the main hall.

> ORTEGO
> Sir?

> ROSS
> Show him the way out! We'll fight him outside.

INT. DESERT BASE — COMMAND CENTER — CONTINUOUS

The main hallway goes dark...a bright light floods the shaft revealing the way out.

Hulk follows the illuminated pathway and heads up the tunnel.

EXT. DESERT BASE — OLD DRIVE-IN THEATER — CONTINUOUS

The ground shakes, the screen collapses. Hulk pauses and then leaps.

INT. DESERT BASE — COMMAND CENTER — CONTINUOUS

> ROSS
> Javelin 6, this is C2. He has breached green level.

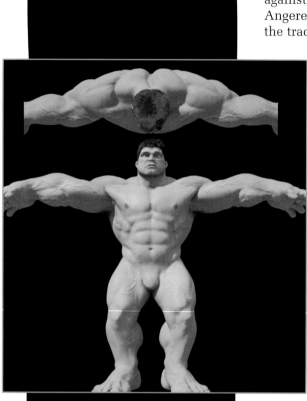

Above: *Early concept art of the veins and muscles of the Hulk served as a guide for consistency of the computer generated character.*

EXT. DESERT BASE — ABANDONED NEIGHBORHOOD
— CONTINUOUS

Hulk lands in the deserted, quiet neighborhood. He sees his old house.

Close: Hulk's eyes.

Above: *Early drawing from the storyboards by Peter Ramsey.* Bottom: *Everything in this scene, except for the telephone pole, the concrete roadway, and the ice cream cone, was matte-painted into the scene by visual effects art director Jules Mann.*

119

Through a window:

The dusty interior of Banner's childhood home.

The sound of the vehicles rises, then recedes for a moment. A ghostly glimpse of the past sweeps through the house—Christmas, 1973—then disappears in the wind.

Then, the whole place erupts in flames, as missile fire lets loose on the entire neighborhood.

A glimpse of Hulk—blasted back by the force of the bombs.

EXT. DESERT DUNES

He lands hard in the dunes, sending up a plume of sand. As he gets up, a group of LAVs, fast-moving desert attack vehicles, close in on him.

He jumps in front of one of them, grabs the chain attached to its bumper. He swings the vehicle around in the air, as a machine gunner fires down in circles around him.

Hulk flings the buggy as the soldiers drop out of it.

The buggy lands on one of the Abrams tanks that are fast approaching, blasting huge amounts of firepower.

Hulk gets to the tank. Lifts the gun turret.

Twists off the entire top of the tank.

Pounds it.

Picks up the tank. Soldiers fall out, run away.

Ground troops moving up behind the tanks.

SERGEANT
Pull back!

Back to ROSS:

INT. DESERT COMMAND CENTER — DAY

120

ROSS
(on a Satellite phone)
Be advised this is T-bolt at Desert Lab. Requesting a flash override for POTUS [President of the United States] and the National Security Advisor.

SATCOMM OPERATOR (V.O)
Ohio.

ROSS
Sandusky. I repeat, Sandusky. Authenticate Alpha Whiskey. Sierra Five Five Zero Three.

SATCOMM OPERATOR (V.O)
I copy, Alpha Whiskey Sierra Five Five Zero, wait one.

ROSS
Roger, standing by.

SATCOMM OPERATOR (V.O.)
This is a secure line. Go ahead, please.

ROSS
Mr. President. I have some bad news.

EXT. RIVER — CONTINUOUS

The President on a phone as he stands in the river flyfishing:

PRESIDENT
Let's have it, General.

INT. LIMOUSINE — CONTINUOUS

The National Security Advisor on a phone:

NATIONAL SECURITY ADVISOR
I have briefed the President on Angry Man. I assume that's what this is about.

Back to Ross:

ROSS
It is, ma'am. I'm requesting National Command Authority override—Angry Man is unsecure, and I need everything we have at my disposal to stop his movement.

NATIONAL SECURITY ADVISOR
General, you expecting civilian casualties?

ROSS
Not if I can help it.

PRESIDENT
Consider it done. Keep us posted.

A VERY LARGE SANDBOX

We had an entire sequence blocked out where Hulk tries to escape from the military. Originally we created complicated storyboards with all these cool ideas about the gadgets the military would use against the Hulk. A few weeks before we shot that scene Ang walked around the actual set and watching him was like seeing the kid inside his head. He was saying, "If I were the Hulk I'd jump up on that, I'd take that thing and throw that over here, and this I'd use as a Frisbee." He completely changed everything we'd planned. Instead of making all these complicated gadgets, Ang showed us that Hulk is a little boy playing with the military in a very large sand box.

I don't understand how Ang Lee can be so calm all the time. I've never heard him yell. He commands such a presence on the set that even when he is directing a crew of 150 people, he doesn't have to raise his voice. People have tremendous respect for him. He's incredibly brilliant but at the same time he's also very humble and I think this makes people want to go the extra mile.

Colin Brady,
Animation Director

GENERAL ROSS
Yes, sir. T-bolt out.

EXT. DESERT BASE — CONTINUOUS

Ross boards a waiting Command and Control Black-hawk.

EXT. DESERT — CONTINUOUS

Hulk begins to run into the desert.

Right: *Concept drawing by Robert MacKenzie of the amount of dirt on the Hulk as he runs through the southwest desert scenes. For every change in environment, a dirt chart was drawn to guide ILM artists. For these desert scenes, ILM artists rolled around in sand and then photographed themselves to chart the amount of dirt that accumulated on their skin and clothes.*

SA
Stage 5. SA93

☐ sand   ☐ heavy sand   ☐ scorch marks

INT. BLACKHAWK — CONTINUOUS

Ross looks down as Hulk takes a running jump. Catches glimpses of green, leaping away.

EXT. DESERT — CONTINUOUS

Hulk runs: picks up speed.

Faster.

INT. BLACKHAWK — CONTINUOUS

ROSS watches on a monitor in amazement as the green figure disappears off the screen.

The BLACKHAWK arches across the sky racing towards Hulk's direction.

> ROSS
> (to Technician #3)
> Contact Goodman control.
> (to Technician #2)
> Patch data to the assets.
> (to Technician #3)
> Contact HQ...have them initiate an immediate evacuation. In the vicinity of grid coordinate 653-216.

> TECHNICIAN #1 (O.S.)
> 3-D Battle space coming up on line now. Target is heading west, bearing 280 degrees.

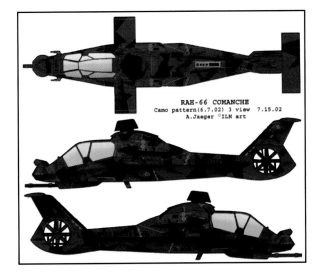

Above: The helicopters in the desert scenes are based on high-tech copters, described by artist Jules Mann as "tanks in the air." These CG copters were used in the desert scenes depicted in the film stills on these pages. Commanche paint concept by ILM artist Alex Jaeger.

HULK FANS

For about a year and a half now, I have been telling people that I'm working on the Hulk and they always say, "What is there to do? It's just a big green guy." And, you know, at first we thought it was going to be our only challenge, to make a well-known comic book hero come to life. But we discovered that creating a CG actor who has to be completely convincing and convey the nuanced performance that Ang expects, demanded that we take our work to a level of subtlety we have not seen before.

For example, one of our first assignments was to visualize the inside of Hulk's mind. This exercise moved us away from the obvious—working on what he looked like when he punched a tank or jumped a mile. Instead, Ang directed us inside the head of the Hulk to get us to understand what it feels like in his psyche. What does rage look like?

I tell the Hulk fans not to worry. Ang is on their side. Hopefully, when they see this movie, they'll recognize all the aspects of the Hulk that they loved from the comic, as well as discover new layers of the Hulk they've never seen before or imagined. If they experience both, we'll have done our job.

Wilson Tang,
Visual Effects Art Director

LANDSCAPES

Ang was extremely interested in the Americana of this film, for the landscapes as well as the characters. He was OK with mixing things up: a mesa from Monument Valley combined with the Moab and then jumping over to Four Corners. He's really trying to create a kind of summary of the Southwest for the audience. Elsewhere in the film, up in the Sierras, he picked an incredibly remote and beautiful location for the end of the film. It took two days just to hike up there, shoot, and come back. We used our PanaScan to get a 360 degree view of the real location from many different views. There's no way to shoot up there; it's something like 9,000 feet up and even a helicopter can't land there. We're all doing it with virtual photography. We went up and shot a lot of still photos and we're creating a virtual location here at ILM.

Dennis Muren,
Visual Effects Supervisor

EXT. DESERT

Four Comanche helicopters in flight.

EXT. DESERT — SOUTHWEST LANDSCAPE

We move with the Hulk.

His breathing.

The landscape swimming by.

Frantic, determined movement, but also a momentary feeling of calm.

INTERCUT TO ROSS:

> ROSS
> Gentleman, it's time to dig in. I want this target stopped in his tracks.

EXT. SOUTHWEST LANDSCAPE — CONTINUOUS

A landscape of steep cliffs and rock formations. Hulk leaps to the top of a formation, looks out over the rocky expanse.

Left: *Storyboard art drawn in a comic book style by Rodolfo Damaggio.*

Momentary, eerie silence.

As he stands there, the four choppers instantly rise from the valley below, hover directly in front of him.

Hulk swiftly reaches out, grabs one of the moving propellers on the closest chopper. As it swings into him, he wrestles its tail. Together, the chopper and Hulk roll down the side of the cliff.

The other choppers dash about, regroup, as Hulk picks himself up and starts climbing.

Hulk dashes across various embankments, cliffs, ravines.

EXT. SOUTHWEST LANDSCAPE — CONTINUOUS

Hulk clambers up a canyon wall, as the Comanches blast away on his tail.

ROSS witnesses the battle. Hulk destroys two of the Comanche helicopters. The remaining two turn and empty all of their available weapons at the Hulk in a huge hail of gunfire. Hulk disappears under a gigantic pile of rock and debris.

The three helicopters hover over the pile of lifeless rubble as the dust clears.

> TANGO-ONE
> T-Bolt, this is Tango-one. We're
> bingo for fuel and ammo. RTB.

EXT. DESERT SKY — DAY

Ross's Blackhawk departs the area, in the distance the High Bird C-130 can be seen descending over the target area.

EXT. DESERT FLOOR — DAY

The dust continues to settle on the pile...a small rock tumbles down the mountain of debris causing a small avalanche. Green skin can be seen...as we zoom in we see it is pulsing, breathing, suddenly...BOOM...the rock pile explodes sending rock and debris sailing through the air like a meteor shower.

EXT. VARIOUS SOUTHWEST LANDSCAPES — CONTINUOUS

Hulk breaks out of landscape and begins a series of enormous leaps.

> HIGH BIRD (V.O)
> Be advised target not destroyed...he's
> on the move again.

> ROSS
> (looking at his monitor)
> I've got it!...It appears he's heading
> home.
> (to Technician #3)
> Contact Goodman control...launch fast
> movers...have them intercept and
> engage.
> (pause)
> Inform them that we'll be on station
> after we refuel.

Original storyboard art that was created in a comic book style at the request of director Ang Lee. Top: Art by Michael Jackson. *Bottom:* Art by Peter Ramsey. *Far right:* Art by Rodolfo Damaggio.

More Hulk leaps. Again, a brief moment of peace, high in the clouds, then down again.

KABOOM!

AARRRRGGHH!!

EXT. JOINT TACTICAL FORCE WEST — FRONT GATE
— DAY

Betty gets a call on her cell phone.

> BETTY ROSS
> Yes.

Intercut Ross:

> ROSS
> Betty. Bruce got out. He's coming your
> way, probably right to you. How far from
> base are you?

> BETTY ROSS
> I'm already here. They're taking his father
> in right now.

> ROSS
> That's all good news. Stay there, Betty.

The small convoy enters the gate.

EXT. JOINT TACTICAL FORCE WEST — JAIL — DAY

The convoy comes to a stop outside the Brig. MPs lead The
Father inside. He smiles, turns, and holds his manacled
hands up to Betty in a gesture of farewell

EXT. SIERRA NEVADAS — CONTINUOUS

HE'S ON THE MOVE AGAIN

SHOOTING IN SEQUOIA NATIONAL PARK

The Hulk was the first production to film in Sequoia National Park, a breathtaking, primal spot studded with streams and lakes and the imposing, inspiring namesake trees. Aside from the locale's natural beauty, the trees provided obvious markers by which to compare the Hulk's immense size. At this picturesque place, the Hulk scoops up Betty Ross. This required stunt coordinator Charlie Croughwell to create an ingenious contraption.

"We figured it would be similar to a puppet on strings, like a marionette, except the puppet we manipulated was a human body, Jennifer Connelly, on a wire. We had her flying from an overhead rig and I had lines in my fingers. I controlled her rotation and her bounce with those lines, almost like a set of reins, which were manned by five crew members. We tested the rig with a double on stage so by the time we got Jennifer there, I knew what the movement should be and only had to fine-tune it a bit on the day," Croughwell explains.

Croughwell practiced with Connelly on the stage before shooting the scene in the sequoias and Connelly adeptly nailed working in the sling inside of forty-five minutes.

Hulk moving. Now, three top-secret Raptor F-22 jets rise up on Hulk's tail.

> F-22 PILOT
> Dash 2 rolling in hot lock and Fox 3. Breaking off left.

> ROSS
> Check fire, check fire. The area's too populated now. We've got to get him out to sea, and terminate him there, over.

EXT. MARIN HEADLANDS — CONTINUOUS

Hulk lands on the Marin headlands, overlooking the Golden Gate Bridge and the city.

The jets buzz him.

INT./EXT. JOINT TACTICAL FORCE WEST — CAPTAIN'S NEST — CONTINUOUS

Betty witnesses the scene from the island.

EXT. GOLDEN GATE BRIDGE

Hulk jumps atop one of the arches of the Golden Gate Bridge. He looks down.

As the planes circle back, one of them flies in low. Ahead of it: a helicopter.

The pilot veers in order to avoid the helicopter, and heads straight into the bridge.

Hulk sees the impending disaster.

Hulk jumps onto the plane, which now dips and swoops just below the bridge, Hulk clinging onto it. Hulk's back scrapes the bottom of the bridge, creasing it, as it passes under.

ROSS

OK, you've got him—now take him on a ride to the top of the world. Let's see what some thin air will do to him.

The plane goes vertical, flies straight up.

I/E. F-22 — CONTINUOUS

Hulk clings to the plane as it rises. Up through the clouds. Ice. Hulk begins to lose consciousness.

Hulk's face, staring into the eyes of the pilot through the cockpit windshield.

His eyes close.

As the plane tilts back, he slides off.

He falls and falls.

A kaleidoscope of images—Hulk's unconscious.

A dreamscape: We cut back to the images we saw near the beginning of the film, now weirdly uncanny:

Banner, in front of a mirror, shaving.

The scrape of the razor.

Watching himself, in the mirror.

Scraping. Slow. The sound.

From inside the mirror, different eyes, watching him.

He stops. Leans closer into the mirror, studying.

Top: *Storyboard art by Rodolfo Damaggio*. Below left: *Art by Michael Jackson depicts a scene shot in the redwood forest.*

CLOSER COVERAGE·
OVER HULK to BANNER ...

OVER BANNER + HULK AS HULK
LASHES OUT + GRABS BANNER ...

HULK GRABS BANNER, PULLING
HIM CLOSER ...

"PUNY HUMAN"

Above: *Storyboard art by Peter Ramsey. The storyboards were created very early in the production of the film.* Right: *Art by Michael Jackson.*

Suddenly, the glass flies apart. Hulk's hand reaches out and takes him by the neck, smashing his face back into the mirror.

Banner, bloodied but unbowed, staring back into Hulk's furious face now, the two of them nose to nose.

They regard each other.

Slowly, Banner raises his hand, gently untwines Hulk's fingers from around his neck.

But just as we think Hulk has calmed, his fingers form a fist: with a quick blow to the face, he snaps Banner's neck back — broken.

On the sound of the break, back to the action:

EXT. SAN FRANCISCO BAY — CONTINUOUS

Hulk crashes into the bay.

He swiftly drops to the floor of the bay, half his body lodged in the muddy bottom, half-conscious.

Betty watches the water.

ROSS's helicopter flies over the bay; he also surveys the huge perturbations across the water.

On the water's surface: nothing.

But then, Hulk is up for air.

EXT. SAN FRANCISCO BAY — UNDERWATER — CONTINUOUS

Hulk drops, deep.

Hits the floor of the bay, bullets flying around him, kicks into gear.

He's on the edge of the city, spots underwater drains, flowing into the bay. He swims into them.

INT. BLACKHAWK

Back to Ross:

F-22 PILOT (V.O.)
T-Bolt, be advised we're gonna cause a lot of damage if we have to start shooting in downtown San Francisco....

ROSS
Roger.
   (beat)
You are still cleared to fire on the target, Legend.

F-22 PILOT (V.O.)
All units are weapons hot....

Ross's face: grim.

Intercut Betty, who has been listening in on the radio exchanges:

BETTY
Dad.

ROSS
Betty, I don't know what choice I have. I have to destroy him.

BETTY
You can't. It will only fuel his rage and make him stronger....

ROSS
He's coming for you, Betty.

BETTY ROSS
Then let me go to him, please. Give him the chance to calm down.

Ross ponders.

Storyboard art by Peter Ramsey depicting the havoc the Hulk wreaks on the streets of San Francisco.

Ang Lee directs the troops on location in San Francisco.

EXT. SAN FRANCISCO STREETS — CONTINUOUS

A cable car rings its bell, moves toward Market Street.

We track behind it, following what starts out as a small crack in the street, flowing as a kind of wake in its path.

The cracks become bigger, heaving upward.

Pedestrians start to notice, jump out of the way.

Water mains begin to break. At each fire hydrant, the caps fly off, water begins to spout.

EXT. JOINT TACTICAL FORCE WEST — CONTINUOUS

Ross's chopper on the tarmac. Betty runs toward it, enters.

It takes off.

Real helicopters were used in the scenes where we see Jennifer Connelly or Sam Elliott. Elements such as the breaking-up of the street (far left) were matte-painted into the scene by Jules Mann.

COORDINATION

If you're going to fly Eric Bana or Hulk through the air, you have to really think about movement. Specifically, I mean how the actor moves in relationship to the way the Hulk will move when the animators start working on him. You have to see a little piece of the Hulk in the real guy and a little bit of the real guy in the Hulk, so there is a real fine coordination between the CG animators and the stunt department. We spend a lot of time teaching movement to the actors.

When the Hulk stomps into San Francisco, the street underneath him is supposed to erupt and everyone should react accordingly. Yet when we are filming, no eruption is actually happening. We were flipping cars and tipping over trolleys and people were falling off so it was a complicated piece of business between the CGI folks and the special effects department.

Charlie Croughwell,
Stunt Coordinator

INT. WATER DRAINS — CONTINUOUS

With each step, Hulk pushes up with his elbows, punching his way through. Finally, he pokes his head through a manhole cover into the light of day.

EXT. SAN FRANCISCO STREETS — CONTINUOUS

A steep intersection, with steps leading down to it from the hill above. Hulk climbs out of the sewer into the middle of the street.

Panic as he stands, momentarily stunned, people tearing away from him in all directions, military and police running towards him, and taking up positions. Hulk

Storyboard art by Rodolfo Damaggio visualizing the Hulk's escape from the underground sewers of San Francisco.

134

CHOPPERS OVERHEAD

The Hulk is set in San Francisco and the company filmed in the city for about three weeks. While there, the production made good use of Terminal Island, the Lawrence Berkeley Laboratory and the surrounding Berkeley campus, an industrial Oakland neighborhood, and Telegraph Hill (the famed upscale neighborhood of Victorian houses near Coit Tower with a spectacular view of the Bay and a nearly vertical ascent).

In one scene called for in the script, the Hulk makes his way up the steep hillside. To create the disastrous aftermath of such a climb, the production filmed several scenes of chaos for a week: a trolley tipping off of its tracks; a line of cars jumping and flipping and nearly crashing; 400 extras, 35 stunt people (performing as passersby), S.W.A.T. teams and military personnel, all choreographed to respond to the Hulk's passage from the Bay to the hilltop.

The apex of the week's work was a procession of helicopters that proceeded up the hill in pursuit of the Hulk, hovering at the top before their final ascent. This exercise required considerable planning and community outreach because the filmmakers received permission to fly the choppers 75 feet above the ground, considerably lower than the F.A.A. approved height of 500 feet. To do this, the filmmakers had to evacuate the residents.

"The truth is that it's just the law. We couldn't fly a helicopter that low with civilians below us," says producer Larry Franco. "We did everything we could to accommodate the neighbors—we compensated those whose roofs we used, we donated to local charities. We had the top helicopter pilots in the business. It was a legal necessity and precaution to evacuate the neighborhood and ultimately, the shots were successful and safe. The rest of it was just movie stunt work—the ground breaking, cars careening down the hill, stuff like that."

Because the chopper sequence ultimately happened on a Friday when most people were at work, only a handful of inhabitants made their way to the local Chinese restaurant that the production bought out for the "evacuees." The remainder took photos and videos of the choppers from the base of the hill. As for the production, four cameras on the ground and one airborne Spacecam captured the action.

"San Francisco is a beautiful city with many layers and I always wanted to make a movie there, it's been one of my dreams," Ang Lee says. "It is amazingly cinematic and romantic and I hope we honored it."

roars at them. In the sky, a fleet of Apaches; on the ground, National Guard, hundreds of soldiers and police; on nearby buildings, Swat teams and snipers: No one is nearer than 200 feet.

But then: Down the steps, Betty slowly walks.

EXT. BLACKHAWK — SAN FRANCISCO STREET

Ross stands by his chopper, now landed, speaking into his radio.

>ROSS
>All units. Hold your fire.
>(beat)
>Let's set her down over there.

EXT. SAN FRANCISCO STREET — DAY

Betty approaches.

Hulk sees her, drops to his knees, lets out a cry of pain and shame.

She comes closer.

Hulk winces, but she comes to him, touches him.

She touches him.

137

Hulk's body begins to contract. Moisture, fluids emerge from every pore as he returns back to Banner.

The crowd — reaction. Silence, and the noise of the choppers and hovering planes.

Banner's face — looking now at Betty.

> BRUCE BANNER
> (exhausted half-smile)
> You found me.

> BETTY ROSS
> (a quick glance around)
> You weren't that hard to
> find.

She starts to cry.

Wide shot: The two of them, clinging to each other, surrounded in the wreckage by troops, police, choppers, the crowd.

INT. JOINT TACTICAL FORCE — BRIG — NIGHT

Father sits in chains. A soldier unlocks his cell. He rises.

INT. JOINT TACTICAL FORCE WEST — HANGAR — NIGHT

A makeshift prison for Banner. He sits on a cot at the end of the hangar, lit by klieg lights. Huge electromagnetic arrays face him, ready to incinerate him at a moment's notice.

His face: calm, contemplative, ready for the end.

EXT. JOINT TACTICAL FORCE WEST — HANGAR — CONTINUOUS

Banner on video monitors, next to communications trucks. ROSS, Betty, others.

> ROSS
> Here's the deal. He stays on the base here until we get final word from C3 on how to dispose of him. Meanwhile, if he does anything but sit there in that chair—we turn up the juice and he's incinerated immediately.

> COLONEL
> We've established a 200-yard perimeter, sir. If we deploy the electromagnetic array, there should be no collateral damage.

> ROSS
> I'm doing this for you Betty…but one way or another, we're going to have to prepare for the worst.

Soldiers at the controls. Tense, hair-triggers.

A personnel transport pulls up. Guards jump down, open

PREPARE FOR THE WORST

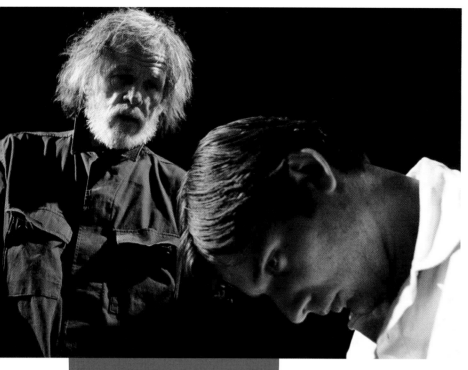

the back. The Father, in chains, is led out of the vehicle, escorted in front of the troops.

He passes by Betty and ROSS. Makes eye contact, but says nothing.

His escorts point him toward the open end of the hangar.

INT. JOINT TACTICAL FORCE WEST — HANGAR — CONTINUOUS

Banner, half-blinded by the lights, sits up, seeing his father's figure come toward him.

Slowly, The Father walks forward, the length of the hangar. Stands before his son. Hangs his head.

Banner, speaking almost in a whisper:

> BRUCE BANNER
> I should have killed you.

> FATHER
> As I should have killed you.

> BRUCE BANNER
> I wish you had.

Banner sinks down onto the cot, his head in his hands.

> BRUCE BANNER (CONT'D)
> I saw her last night. In my mind's eye. I saw her face. Brown hair, brown eyes. She smiled at me, she leaned down and kissed my cheek. I can almost remember a smell, like desert flowers—

> FATHER
> —Her favorite perfume.

> BRUCE BANNER
> My mother. I don't even know her name.

Bruce starts to cry.

Intercut:

Betty and ROSS, watching on the monitors. The sound is low, distorted, but they can just make out the conversation.

> FATHER
> (nervously playing with a nearby lamp cord)
> That's good. Crying will do you good.

CRYING WILL DO YOU GOOD

Far right: *Visual effects art director Wilson Tang's concept art showing cell growth and nanomeds entering the cells, causing cellular healing. Nanomeds are among the production's invented technological explanations for how the Hulk grows.*

He walks toward his son, reaches out with his manacled hands.

> BRUCE BANNER
>
> No. Please don't touch me. Maybe, once,
> you were my father. But you're not now—
> you never will be.

> FATHER
>
> (beat)
> Is that so? Well, I have news for you. I
> didn't come here to see you. I came for
> my son.

Bruce looks up at him, confused.

> FATHER (CONT'D)
>
> My real son—the one inside of you. You
> are merely a superficial shell, a husk of
> flimsy consciousness, surrounding him,
> ready to be torn off at a moment's notice.

> BRUCE BANNER
>
> Think whatever you like. I don't care. Just
> go now.

The Father smiles, laughs. Whispers:

> FATHER
>
> But Bruce—I have found a cure—for me.
> (beat—now more menacing) You see, my
> cells too can transform—absorb enormous
> amounts of energy, but unlike you, they're
> unstable. Bruce, I need your strength. I
> gave you life, now you must give it back
> to me—only a million times more radiant,
> more powerful.

> BRUCE BANNER
>
> Stop.

> FATHER
>
> Think of it—all those men out there, in
> their uniforms, barking and swallowing
> orders, inflicting their petty rule over the
> globe, think of all the harm they've done,
> to you, to me—and know we can make
> them and their flags and anthems and
> governments disappear in a flash. You—
> in me.

> BANNER
>
> I'd rather die.

> FATHER
>
> And indeed you shall. And be reborn a
> hero of the kind that walked the earth
> long before the pale religions of civiliza-
> tion infected humanity's soul.

Bruce Banner leaps up, screaming.

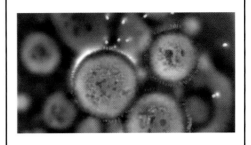
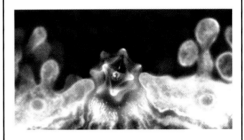
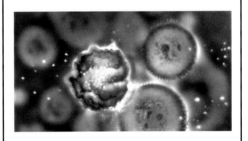
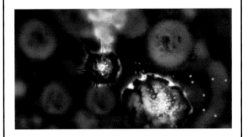
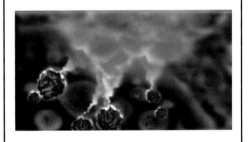

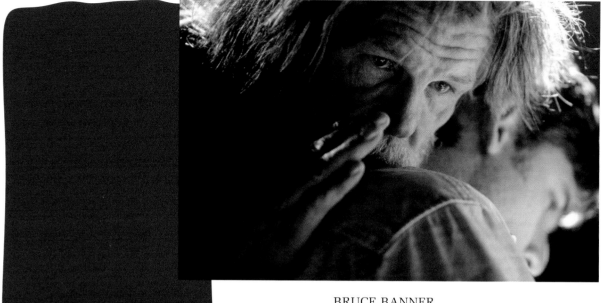

BRUCE BANNER

Go!

Intercut:

ROSS, the soldiers: about to detonate.

FATHER

Stop your bawling, you weak little speck
of human debris. I'll go.

He grabs one of the thick electrical cables lining the floor,
tears it apart.

FATHER (CONT'D)

Just watch me go!

The live wires sputter—and then he takes them into his
mouth.

Concept art by Alex Jaeger is meant to show size, scale, brightness, and other elements that cause the Father to absorb electricity and take on some of its properties.

The lights in the hangar begin to sputter.

Banner rises, a glimpse of green already showing in his eyes.

> BRUCE BANNER
> No!

He jumps toward The Father, but is bounced back by the current.

Back to Ross:

> ROSS
> What the hell!

The soldier at the controls, nervous, pulls the switch.

The electromagnetic arrays come to life: We feel a burst of enormous energy surging from them.

But instead of irradiating out, their energy flows directly into the outstretched arms of The Father.

EXT. JOINT TACTICAL FORCE WEST — HANGAR — CONTINUOUS

From above, we see the lights on the island, then on the bridges, then throughout the entire Bay Area, in a wave, go out.

INT. JOINT TACTICAL FORCE WEST — HANGAR — CONTINUOUS

The Father, his body coursing with electrical energy.

His shackles crackle and break open.

The arrays, in a flash, implode.

The Father flings out his arms, sending up an electromagnetic field that makes the entire hangar sizzle.

EXT. JOINT TACTICAL FORCE WEST — HANGAR — CONTINUOUS

The monitors—all dark. Now even the headlights and ignitions on the vehicles sputter out.

> ROSS
> Hit them again!

> SOLDIER
> We can't, sir. There's no power, some kind of counter electromagnetic field—

> ROSS
> Then move in there—with everything you've got. Fire at will.

The Father, laughing, looks over at where Bruce was thrown—and is met by a huge green fist which lifts him, in a lightning flash, into the air, through the roof of the hangar and across the bay. The Hulk, with a roar, leaps after him.

EXT. MOUNTAIN LAKE SUMMIT — CONTINUOUS

The Father and the Hulk, in a firestorm of electricity, land by the water's edge of a distant mountain lake.

They rise and face each other. The Father now stands almost as tall as the Hulk, the electricity now drained from his body, laughing.

Above: *Concept art by Jules Mann of the electric Father in flight. Top right: Concept art by Wilson Tang of the underwater fight between the Hulk and The Father. Below right: Concept art by Jules Mann of The Father when he is transformed into rock, an image that was meant to somewhat resemble Nick Nolte.*

The Hulk roars at The Father.

EXT. JOINT TACTICAL FORCE WEST — HANGAR — CONTINUOUS

The sound registers on one of the monitors at Ross's command center.

TECHNICIAN
Sir, I've got them
on radar. Pear
Lake.

ROSS
Call up the task
force.

EXT. MOUNTAIN
LAKE SUMMIT —
NIGHT

Under a full moon.

Hulk, with both fists,
pounds into The Father.

Father takes each blow
—and with each blow,
he seems to grow big-
ger, greener—absorbing
Hulk's energy, cellular
structure.

Hulk steps back, re-
gards him, horrified, as
The Father stands, as
big as Hulk now.

Hulk, confused now,
keeps his distance—
about to strike, but
holds back.

Then, he crouches
down, and, scooping
up an enormous boul-
der, lifts it and lets it
crash down on The
Father.

He pounds away, again and again, as the Father turns
to stone.

A final blow, and The Father breaks up into a small
mountain of dust and rock fragments; they fall upon
Hulk, who pushes them off, but in so doing he trans-
fers enough energy back to The Father so that he re-
shapes.

Now Hulk, in a fury, lashes out once again with his
fists. The two of them, locked in struggle, make their
way to the lake's edge, wildly pounding away at each
other.

With each blow, the air around them seems to grow
colder, vacant. Even the water begins to turn opaque,
icy.

The two of them seem almost to merge as the lake's
water begins to freeze around them.

EXT. JOINT TACTICAL FORCE WEST — HANGAR — NIGHT

Ross and Betty at monitors.

> OFFICER
> Strange.

Satellite images: zooming in.

> OFFICER (CONT'D)
> We're reading…a phenomenal drop in temperatures there, but simultaneous radiological activity.

> BETTY ROSS
> The ambient energy—they're absorbing it all.

EXT. SKY — NIGHT

Fighter jets flying.

I/E. FROZEN MOUNTAIN LAKE SUMMIT — NIGHT

The two enormous figures, locked in a death grip, frozen in the lake bed.

We circle around them, then into the layers of ice, sparks of energy—neural charges—spiking through the frozen water.

Smash inside the Hulk's frozen eyes.

Through the retina, the neural pathways—back into the space of his unconscious we saw back at Desert Base.

Thousands of images, bits of memory and desire, suddenly coalescing into a moment of absolute calm, and clarity.

Above: Concept art by Wilson Tang of The Father as flowing water. This very early, preliminary image was proposed but not used in the film. Below: Concept art by Jules Mann of The Father's image on the surface of the lake which leads to a key point of the story: The Father in jellyfish form as seen (top right) in Tang's concept art.

Flashback:

The ice begins to crack.

From the melting ice, The Father rises, lifts Hulk's fist, holds it to his stomach.

Hulk—struggling—but his strength is going, he's shrinking, as The Father takes the last of him.

Hulk seems to dissolve, but we catch a brief glimpse of Banner, inside the dropping shape, as it falls into the lake.

The Father, victorious, towering above the mountains, sees in the

horizon a fleet of puny stealth fighters and jet formations making their way toward him.

He laughs, his laughter resounding like thunder.

But now The Father pauses, amid his laughter, and looks down at his stomach—swirling energy, radiating into his whole body, making it bigger, bigger.

He thrashes, looking for Banner/Hulk, begins to howl.

He stumbles to the top of the mountain.

We see the fighter planes swiftly approaching in the background.

EXT. JOINT TACTICAL FORCE WEST — COMMAND CENTER — CONT. — NIGHT

ROSS looks at his daughter as he gives his final order.

> ROSS
> Gentlemen, release.

Back at the mountain:

A huge thermonuclear bomb takes off from one of the planes, heading straight for the Father, who continues to grow and distend in an agony of energy.

The missile strikes him. From within, a massive explosion—eerily, the gamma explosion from Banner and Betty's memories—engulfs the sky.

EXT. JOINT TACTICAL FORCE WEST — COMMAND CENTER — CONT. — NIGHT

On the monitors: explosion.

ROSS, grim, drops his face into his hands.

A hand on his shoulder. He looks up: Betty.

I/E. PLANE — CONTINUOUS — NIGHT

The planes pull back and away.

The winds rise to the heavens. A stillness descends on the forest valleys below: The Father is gone forever.

A glimpse of the bottom of the lake—Banner's body lying on the lake bed. Alive or dead?

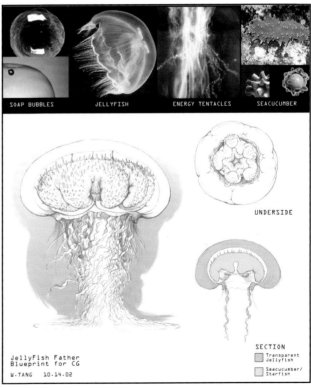

Above: *Wilson Tang's chart for the jellyfish image. The Father as jellyfish echoes the very first shot in the movie of a jellyfish and combines both the science and the metaphor of Banner's anger taking on a tangible form, suggestive of both a jellyfish and a nuclear mushroom cloud.*

149

BOXES OF ROCKS

Before Ang Lee arrived at the ILM studios in northern California, he shipped out twenty-four boxes of rocks. The rocks were unpacked and polished though no one at ILM quite knew where they would be used in the production of the movie.

The staff at ILM was surprised to learn that the rocks were not meant for filming. Ang Lee began collecting the rocks from various locations he visited in preparation for filming *The Hulk.* In addition, the director collected pieces of driftwood, sand, an array of starfish and sea urchins, and various examples of dried moss and lichen. All of it was shipped back to ILM. In a spare room, next to his office, the director covered every surface with his rocks and other organic materials chosen for their color or texture.

The spare room functions as a kind of sanctuary for the director. "He removes his shoes and uses the room for inspiration," marvels ILM artist Jules Mann. "We are really learning a lot from Ang Lee."

Concept art by Robert MacKenzie of the Father transformed into rock.

INT. BETTY'S NEW LAB — DAY

Close up: twisted strands of DNA, magnified under the lens of a microscope.

Title:

ONE YEAR LATER—

MUTAGENIC TRACES—BUT OF WHAT?

Months later. Betty, contemplative, alone, looking through a microscope.

In the lens: twisted strands of DNA.

The phone rings.

> ROSS (V.O.)
> Betty, that you?

> BETTY
> Hi, Dad.

> ROSS
> I'm glad I caught you.

> BETTY
> I'm glad you called.

> ROSS
> Thanks...You and I, well...we both know that Bruce, he couldn't have survived that blast, but—

> BETTY
> —Dad, what is it?

> ROSS
> You know, the usual loonies, people seeing things, only now everything's green.

> BETTY ROSS
> (laughs)
> Right.

> ROSS
> I know this goes without saying, but if, and I say if, by any chance, he should contact you, try to get in touch, you'd tell me now, wouldn't you?

> BETTY
> No...I wouldn't. You know as well as I do I wouldn't have to. My phones are bugged, I'm under surveillance. I can tell you, if he were alive, I'm the last person I'd want him to come to. Because as much as I miss him, I love him.

> ROSS
> I'm so sorry, Betty.

BETTY

I know.

She looks out her window, a couple of trees at the end of the parking lot, swaying slightly.

EXT. JUNGLE CLEARING — DAY

Palm trees thrash around in a stiff wind. Wind lashes a makeshift canvas-covered shelter. Three white-clad Red Cross workers are tending to a few rural families; kids, their parents, grandparents.

One of the Red Cross workers is a man wearing longish hair and a beard. He examines an eight-year-old boy, being held lovingly by his father, who looks feverish, glassy-eyed, and slack. The worker looks at the boy's father and pulls a pill bottle out of his kit.

Note: all dialogue in this scene is in Spanish.

RED CROSS WORKER

You need to give him this three times a day, for ten days, OK?

BOY'S FATHER

Gracias.

RED CROSS WORKER
(to the boy)

You listen to your father, when he tells you to take this medicine, OK?

151

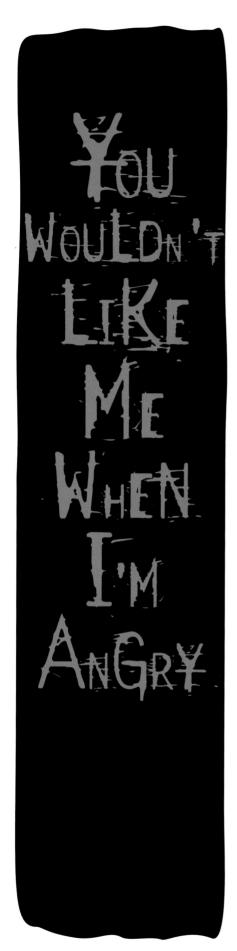

YOU WOULDN'T LIKE ME WHEN I'M ANGRY

BOY

Si.

The boy smiles at his father, who smiles back at him.

The other Red Cross Worker, a pretty young local girl, looks for the next person in line, but sees a group of heavily armed men coming out of the jungle. A look of concern crosses her face. She gestures to the next child in line, and smiles reassuringly.

The armed men come into the tent, driving the locals out, laying down, and rifling through the supplies.

RED CROSS WORKER

We need these medicines for the people who live here.

PARAMILITARY

Who are you to say what is needed, foreigner? These people are helping our enemies. And maybe so are you.

He grabs the medicine kit.

PARAMILITARY (CONT'D)

We need these, too. They are now the property of the government.

The paramilitary pushes a child out into the rain and raises his AK-47. His men stand up and gather around him menacingly.

RED CROSS WORKER

You shouldn't of done that. Now say you're sorry and get out of here.

The paramilitaries raise their eyebrows, giggle.

PARAMILITARY

What?

RED CROSS WORKER

You're making me angry.

He looks up.

Close: Banner's eyes:

BANNER

You wouldn't like me when I'm angry.

Pull up and away, high above the jungle, an unbroken sea of green.

END.

152

UNIVERSAL PICTURES Presents

In Association with MARVEL ENTERPRISES

A VALHALLA MOTION PICTURES /
GOOD MACHINE Production

An ANG LEE Film

THE HULK

ERIC BANA

JENNIFER CONNELLY

SAM ELLIOTT

JOSH LUCAS

and NICK NOLTE

Casting by
AVY KAUFMAN, C.S.A.
Music by
DANNY ELFMAN
Costume Designer
MARIT ALLEN
Associate Producers
DAVID WOMARK
CHERYL A. TKACH
Visual Effects Producer
TOM PEITZMAN
Visual Effects Supervisor
DENNIS MUREN, A.S.C.
Animation Supervisor
COLIN BRADY
Editor
TIM SQUYRES, A.C.E.
Production Designer
RICK HEINRICHS
Director of Photography
FREDERICK ELMES, A.S.C
Executive Producers
STAN LEE
KEVIN FEIGE
Produced by
GALE ANNE HURD
AVI ARAD
Produced by
JAMES SCHAMUS
LARRY FRANCO
Story by
JAMES SCHAMUS
Screenplay by
JOHN TURMAN and
MICHAEL FRANCE and
JAMES SCHAMUS
Directed by
ANG LEE
Unit Production Manager
DAVID WOMARK
First Assistant Director
ARTIST ROBINSON
Second Assistant Director
DEANNA STADLER
Second Second Assistant Director
MARIA BATTLE CAMPBELL

Based on the Marvel Comic Book
Character Created by
STAN LEE and JACK KIRBY
"Set Me Free"
Written and Performed by
SCOTT WEILAND, SLASH, DUFF MCKAGAN,
MATT SORUM and DAVE KUSHNER
Produced by
NICK RASKULINECZ

CAST

Bruce Banner	ERIC BANA
Betty Ross	JENNIFER CONNELLY
Ross	SAM ELLIOTT
Talbot	JOSH LUCAS
Father	NICK NOLTE
Young David Banner	PAUL KERSEY
Edith Banner	CARA BUONO
Young Ross	TODD TESEN
Harper	KEVIN RANKIN
Mrs. Krenzler	CELIA WESTON
Teenage Bruce Banner	MIKE ERWIN
Security Guards	LOU FERRIGNO
	STAN LEE
	REGI DAVIS
	CRAIG DAMON
President	GEOFFREY SCOTT
National Security Advisor	REGINA MCKEE REDWING
Aide	DANIEL DAE KIM
Edith's Friend	DANIELLA KUHN
Bruce Banner as Child	MICHAEL AND DAVID KRONENBERG
Betty Ross as Child	RHIANNON LEIGH WRYN
Pediatrician	LOU RICHARDS
Waitress	JENNIFER GOTZON
Delivery Doctor	LOUANNE KELLEY
Delivery Nurse	TONI KALLEN
Officer	PAUL HANSEN KIM
Security NCO	JOHN LITTLEFIELD
Soldiers	LORENZO CALLENDER
	TODD LEE CORALLI
	JOHNNY KASTL
	ERIC WARE
Colonels	JESSE CORTI
	ROB SWANSON
Technicians	MARK ATTEBERRY, EVA BURKLEY, RONDDA HOLEMAN, JOHN A. MARAFFI, MICHAEL PAPAJOHN, DAVID ST. PIERRE, BONI YANAGISAWA
Tank Commander	DAVID SUTHERLAND
Comanche Pilots	SEAN MAHON
	BRETT THACHER
	KIRK B.R. WOLLER
F-22 Pilot	RANDY NEVILLE
Atheon Technician	JOHN PROSKY
Boy	AMIR FARAJ
Boy's Father	RICARDO AGUILAR
Paramilitary	VICTOR RIVERS
Davey	LYNDON KARP
Stunt Coordinator	CHARLIE CROUGHWELL
Assistant Stunt Coordinator	SCOTT SPROULE

Stunts............ERIC ABRAHAMSON, JONI AVERY, RICK AVERY, GREGG BARNETT, DOTAN BONAN, MARY BOSS, JAKE BRAKE, CRAIG BRANHAM, WENDI BROMLEY, BRADY CONRAD, CALLIE CROUGHWELL, CAMERON CROUGHWELL, JOSHUA CROUGHWELL, MICHELLE CROUGHWELL, COREY EUBANKS, DANE FARWELL, SCOTT FISHER, CLAY FONTENOT, SEAN GRAHAM, KEVIN GREVIOUX, BEVIN KAYE, ANDREW LANTIERI, CLAY LILLEY, CLINT LILLEY, MEGAN MARSHALL, TRISTAN MORTS, WILLIAM MORTS, CASEY O'NEILL, HAILEY PEITZMAN, HANNAH PEITZMAN, MOLLY PEITZMAN, MEGAN ROBINSON, JASON RODRIGUEZ, TOMMY ROSALES, JR., DAVID ROWDEN, MIKA SAITO, GUNTHER SCHLIERKAMP, JESSE TIPTON, SONNY TIPTON, WYATT TIPTON, MARTIN VALINSKY, AVA ROSE WILLIAMS, DARLENE WILLIAMS, JERRY WILLS, GABRIEL WOMARK, MERRITT YOHNKA

ILM Visual Effects Producer..............JANET LEWIN
ILM Visual Effects Co-Supervisor.............ED HIRSH
Special Effects Supervisor.........MICHAEL LANTIERI
Production Supervisor............MICHAEL MALONE
Supervising Art Director................JOHN DEXTER
Art Director.......................GREG PAPALIA
Set Decorator................CHERYL A. CARASIK
A Camera Operator.............DANIEL C. GOLD
B Camera Operator/Steadicam.......TOMMY LOHMANN
Production Sound Mixer................DREW KUNIN
Visual FX Editor......................GARY LEVY
First Assistant Editor (Film)...........DEVON MILLER
First Assistant Editor (Avid).............CRAIG ALPERT
Property Master.....................JERRY MOSS
Construction Coordinator............JOHN W. HOSKINS
Transportation Coordinator......TOMMY TANCHAROEN
Key Grip.........................GARY L. DAGG
Gaffer...........................JIM TYNES
Production Accountant.................KATHY PETTY
Production Coordinator...........JENNIFER CAMPBELL
Script Supervisor.............JAYNE-ANN TENGGREN
Supervising Location Manager..LAURA SODE-MATTESON
Science Consultant.............JOHN UNDERKOFFLER

Sound Design.....................EUGENE GEARTY
GARY RYDSTROM
Supervising Sound Editors...........RICHARD HYMNS
EUGENE GEARTY
Re-Recording Mixers................GARY RYDSTROM
MICHAEL SEMANICK

Assistant Art Directors............MARIKO BRASWELL, CHAD S. FREY, WILL HAWKINS, NORM NEWBERRY
Set Designers.............ROY BARNES, JIM BAYLISS, TODD CHERNIAWSKY, AL HOBBS, LUIS G. HOYOS, KRISTEN PRATT, PATTE STRONG-LORD, DON WOODRUFF

Storymatic Illustrators.................PETER RAMSEY
RODOLFO DAMAGGIO
MICHAEL ANTHONY JACKSON
Illustrators........MAURO BORRELLI, JAMES CARSON, JAMES MARTIN, CHRIS ROSS
Animatic.........................JAMES ROTHWELL
3-D Set Model Builder................DAVID Y. CHOW
Graphic Designer....................SUSAN A. BURIG
Art Department Coordinator.........KIRSTIN MOONEY
Art Department Assistants...........ETHAN GOODWIN
JONAS MAYABB
LISA JACKSON
1st Assistant A Camera...............TREVOR LOOMIS
2nd Assistant A Camera..........RODNEY SANDOVAL
1st Assistant B Camera.................KEITH DAVIS
Loader.......................MARK CONNELLY
Remote Head Operator...................KELLY DIEHL

Aerial Director of Photography...........HANS BJERNO
Aerial Stunt Coordinator..............CRAIG HOSKING
Pilots..........................CLIFF FLEMING
RICK SHUSTER
Video Assist........................BRYCE SHIELDS
Boom Operator..................MARK GOODERMOTE
Utility Sound......................JAMES J. MASE

Visual Effects Coordinator........CHRISTOPHER RAIMO
Video Effects Supervisor.......MATTHEW MORRISSEY
Video Graphics Coordinator...............DAVE HENRI
Chief Computer/Video Engineer..........ALAN PORTER
Computer/Video Engineer...........MATTHEW COHEN
Graphics Production Assistant.......CHARLES TREBINO

Assistant Property Master.......ANDREW D. PETROTTA
Prop Assistant.....................MICHAEL HANSEN
Prop Shop Supervisor.............THOMAS HOMSHER
Leadman.......................ERNEST SANCHEZ
Buyers..........................WENDY WEAVER
KATHLEEN A. ROSEN
Gang Boss...................CRAIG A. ZIMMERMAN
Set Dressers......MARILYN MORGAN, MIKE THURMAN, DEAN LAKOFF, CHRISTOPHER CASEY, CHRISTOPHER KENNEDY

Key Assistant Accountant........GAIL FOREMAN ROSE

Assistant Accountants..................KELLI GILLAM
YVONNE RAYMOND
OOPIE PARRACO
Payroll.........................DAVID ROMANO
TANIA LEVIN
Accounting Assistants.............MARGO ROMANO, JAMES D'AMERY, JR., NICOLE GALLARDO, ABBIE LUDWIG, LESLIE COOGAN, SIMI PETTERMANN

Casting Associate.................MAUREEN WHALEN
Extras Casting.....................BEAU BONNEAU
FRANKLYN WARREN
KIM JU

155

Stills Photographer . . . . PETER SOREL
Unit Publicist . . . . RACHEL ABERLY

Animal Trainer. . . . . ROGER SCHUMACHER
Dialogue Coach . . . . SUSAN HEGARTY
Assistant Production Coordinator . . . MEREDITH HUMBRACHT
Production Secretary. . . . . LISA JOELLE CURTIS
Production Assistants . . . . JENNIFER ROSSINI,
TIM BALL, VENESSA DE ANDA,
MATT RUBIN, MATTHEW W. BRUCELL,
RYAN FAUST, ROBIN MOORE,
PHRONSIE FRANCO, OORALA YAMADA-WALMAN,
DANNY MORMINO, STEVE SIMON,
HANNA HINKEL, JESSICA TATE,
DARREN BLATT, FALLON JOHNSON

Military Consultant . . . . NICK TETA
Comanche Advisor. . . . . JOHN ARMBRUST
F-22 Advisor . . . . RANDY NEVILLE

Key Hair Stylist. . . . . JAN ALEXANDER
Hair Stylist . . . . CAROLYN ELIAS
Key Makeup . . . . DENNIS LIDDIARD
Ms. Connelly's Makeup . . . . BRAD WILDER
Costume Supervisor . . . . PAM WISE
Military Key Costumer . . . . JOE MCCLOSKEY
Key Costumers . . . . NIGEL BOYD
DIANA J. WILSON
Set Costumers . . . . WENDY M. CRAIG
TRICIA BERCSI
Military Set Costumer. . . . . AMANDA GORE
Costumer. . . . . KATHLEEN MISKO

Additional Location Managers . . . . VAL KIM
STEPHEN MAPEL
Assistant Location Manager . . . . PERRI FICHTNER
Location Manager (S.F.) . . . . RORY ENKE
Assistant Location Manager (S.F.). . . . . RICHARD J. MARKS
Assistants to Mr. Lee. . . . . DANNY HUANG
DAVID LEE
Assistant to Ms. Hurd. . . . . TIMOTHY REID
Assistant to Mr. Arad . . . . CHELSEA RUTTER
Assistant to Mr. Schamus. . . . . PETER KUJAWSKI

Best Boy Electric. . . . . CRICKET SLOAT
Universal Best Boy Electric . . . . O'SHANA WALKER

Electricians. . . . . NORMAN ASH, JAMES F. CORNICK,
CHRIS FUNK, RONALD JOSEPH PURE, JR.,
TIM MCDONALD, DAVID SCOTT,
JOHN SKIDMORE
Rigging Gaffer. . . . . FRANK DOROWSKY
Rigging Best Boy Electric . . . . . . CHRISTOPHER BATEMAN
Best Boy Grip. STEELE HUNTER
Dolly Grips . . . . MICHAEL SCHWAKE
DAVID W. NIMMS
Grips . . . . RICK GUERTIN, PETE MCADAMS,
PAUL A. RYCHLEC, RODNEY VETO
Technocrane Technician . . . . . . DERLIN BRYNFORD-JONES
Rigging Key Grip . . . . THOMAS WAZNEY
Rigging Best Boy Grip. . . . . JOSEPH E. BATES

Special Effects Set Foreman . . . . SCOTT FISHER
Special Effects Shop Supervisor . . . . TOM PAHK
Special Effects Shop Foreman . . . . . . DONALD R. ELLIOTT
Special Effects Foreman . . . . BRIAN TIPTON
Special Effects Technicians . . . . RONALD EPSTEIN,
CORY FAUCHER, MARK HAWKER,
RAYMOND HOFFMAN, FRANK IUDICA,
JAY B. KING, LOUIE LANTIERI,
JOEL MITCHELL, RALPH PETERSON,
JAMES S. ROLLINS, WILLIAM SHOURT,
STEVEN SCOTT WHEATLEY, LARRY ZELANAY
SFX Propmakers. ROBIN REILLY
RICHARD ZARRO
RONALD ZARRO

General Foreman . . . . ROBERT LAMBERT
Construction Foreman . . . . CLETE CETRONE

Location Foreman. . . . . JERRY SARGENT
Propmaker Foremen . . . . MICHAEL B. BUNCH,
MICHAEL BURKE, RICHARD D. CRAIN,
FRED DEYOE, JOHN J. GIULIANO,
DEAN E. HENSLEY, HENRY S. JOHN,
MARK KNAPTON, THOMAS LAUFI,
DWIGHT LOWELL, DOUGLASS ROSENBERGER,
HUBERT W. RYAN III, RICHARD VALLONE
Paint Supervisor . . . . CLYDE ZIMMERMAN
Paint Foremen . . . . TIMOTHY ACKERS
CHRIS HERRINGTON
KENT JONES
ROBERT M. MISETICH
DAVE MORALES
Standby Painter . . . . CHRIS ZIMMERMAN
Supervising Plaster Foreman . . . . ROBERT WILBANKS
Plaster Foremen. DAVE KILBY
DOUGLAS R. MILLER
SALVADOR SANCHEZ
Lead Sculptor . . . . JAMES MILLER
Sculptors. . . . . CHRIS C. HOPKINS
JEFF FROST
DEREK C. PENDLETON
Senior Modeler . . . . DAVID COHEN
Model Makers. . . . . MICHAEL BINCZEK,
ANTHONY COPE, MICHAEL N. DUPUIS,
JASON MAHAKIAN, JEFFREY N. MANNING,
EDWARD J. QUINN
Supervising Laborer Foreman . . . . BRIAN ROCK
Laborer Foremen. RON BROWN,
TED CASTRELLON, RICHARD L. CLENDENEN,
ROBERT A. LAUX, JACK LASPADA,
ANTHONY J. MARTIN, RONALD MARTINEZ,
WILLIAM L. WHEATON
Supervising Welder . . . . RUBEN GARCIA
Welding Foreman. . . . . MICHAEL HOLLAND, SR.
Greens Supervisor . . . . DANNY ONDREJKO
Greens Foremen . . . . . . KEVIN MANGAN, CARLO BASAIL,
RICHARD W. JONES, BOB SKEMP,
JEFF THOMAS
Greens Standby. . . . . JOSE LUIS OROZCO

Transportation Captain . . . . LEE GARIBALDI
Transportation Co-Captain . . . . THOMAS WHELPLEY

Picture Car Coordinator .... PAUL STROH
Office Coordinator .... AUDREY A. CONRAD
Catering .... GALA CATERING
Craft Service .... RAY BULINSKI
Post Production Supervisor .... LISA RODGERS
Assistant Editors.................... DIVA MAGPAYO
                                   PEGGY EGHBALIAN
Editorial Assistants................. DAVID MATUSEK
                                     ANTHONY REYNA

Special Visual Effects
and Animation by
INDUSTRIAL LIGHT & MAGIC
a Lucasfilm Ltd. Company
Marin County, California

Computer Graphics
  Supervisors .... CHRISTOPHER TOWNSEND
                           GERALD GUTSCHMIDT
                           MICHAEL DI COMO
Compositing Supervisors .... MARSHALL KRASSER
                                   DORNE HUEBLER
Visual Effects Art Directors.............. WILSON TANG
                                         JULES MANN
Hulk R&D/Sequence Supervisor......... HILMAR KOCH
Technical Animation Supervisor .... SCOTT BENZA
Creature Development Supervisors ... AARON FERGUSON
                                      PAUL GIACOPPO
Animation Sequence Supervisors ..... TIM HARRINGTON
                                     GLEN MCINTOSH
                                     JAMY WHELESS
Associate Producer .... SHARI HANSON
Sequence Supervisors .... PATRICK BRENNAN,
                  IAN CHRISTIE, PATRICK CONRAN,
                  LINDY DEQUATTRO, JOHN HELMS,
                  SEAN MACKENZIE, TOM MARTINEK,
                  TIA MARSHALL, JEFF SUTHERLAND,
                                     DOUG SUTTON
Viewpaint Supervisor .... SUSAN ROSS
Physical Model Supervisor............. STEVE GAWLEY
Animators .... ISMAIL ACAR, GEORGE ALECO-SIMA,
                  CHARLES ALLENECK, SUE CAMPBELL,
                  DERRICK CARLIN, SEAN CURRAN,
                  VIRGINIE D'ANNOVILLE, LOU DELLAROSA,
                  ANDREW DOUCETTE, MICHAEL EASTON,
                  MIGUEL FUERTES, DAVID GAINEY, ANDREW GRANT,
                  MAIA KAYSER, PETER KELLY, SHAWN KELLY,
                  GREG KYLE, DAVID LATOUR, ALISON LEAF,
                  JANICE LEW, KEVIN MARTEL, PHIL MCNALLY,
                  CHRISTOPHER MINOS, RICK O'CONNOR,
                  HIROMI ONO, JAKUB PISTECKY, STEVE RAWLINS,
                  JAY RENNIE, MAGALI RIGAUDIAS, KEVIN SCOTT,
                  DAVE SIDLEY, SHARONNE SOLK, TOM ST. AMAND,
                  TRISH SCHUTZ-KRAUSE, KIM THOMPSON,
                  DELIO TRAMONTOZZI, MARJOLAINE TREMBLAY,
                                     JAN VAN BUYTEN

Motion Capture Tech Animators........ TIM STEVENSON
                                     NEIL LIM SANG
                                     KEVIN WOOLEY
Lead TDs .... MAYUR PATEL
                                     KEVIN REUTER
                                     KEN WESLEY

TDs .... JOAKIM ARNESSON,
            JEAN-PAUL BEAULIEU, SUZANNE BERGER,
            MATTHEW BLACKWELL, MATTHEW BOUCHARD,
                  SAM BREACH, JASON BROWN,
            THOMAS BURNETTE, MARIO CAPELLARI,
            JOSHUA CHAPEL, LEILA CHESLOFF,
            JAY COOPER, KATHLEEN DAVIDSON,
            NATASHA DEVAUD, RICHARD DUCKER,
            JEFFREY ERTL, RAÙL ESSIG, ALEX ETHIER,
                  BRAD FOX, RYAN GALLOWAY,
            GONZALO GARRAMUNO, BRIAN GEE,
            HOWARD GERSH, BRANKO GRUJCIC,
            JEFF HATCHEL, IAN HOUSE, PEG HUNTER,
            POLLY ING, GREGOR LAKNER, DONNA LANASA,
            JEROEN LAPRE, JOSHUA LEBEAU, DANIEL LEUNG,
                  MICHAEL LUDLAM, SAIRA MATHEW,
            KEITH MCCABE, JOSEPH METTEN, MICHAEL MUIR,
            KENNETH NIELSEN, MASI OKA, KHATSHO ORFALI,
                  DANIEL PEARSON, BRUCE POWELL,
            SCOTT PRIOR, RICARDO RAMOS, PHILIPPE REBOURS,
            JASON ROSSON, SABA ROUFCHAIE,
            FREDERIC SCHMIDT, DURANT SCHOON,
                  ANTHONY SHAFER, PAUL SHARPE,
            DOUGLAS JAMES SMITH, NIGEL SUMNER,
            BLAKE SWEENEY, ERIC TEXIER, MEGHAN THORNTON,
            TERRANCE TORNBERG, BARBARA TOWNSEND,
                  ANGELA TRAEGER, KELLY WALSH,
            BRANDON WARNER, DAVID WEITZBERG,
                               RICCARDO ZANETTINI
Creature TDs.................... ANDREW ANDERSON,
                  WILLIAM CLAY, HYUN SEUNG KIM,
            TODD KRISH, LENNY LEE, ANDREA MAIOLO,
            VIJAY MYNENI, TIMOTHY NAYLOR,
            STEVE SAUERS, LEE UREN, ERIC WONG
Compositors .... MIMI ABERS, LEAH ANTON,
            JEFFREY ARNOLD, OKAN ATAMAN,
            KATHLEEN BEELER, BARBARA BRENNAN,
            COLIN CAMPBELL, RAFAEL COLON,
            CAITLIN CONTENT, EMMET DOYLE,
            SAM EDWARDS, BILL EYLER, KELLY FISCHER,
                  TIM GIBBONS, BILL GILMAN,
            ROBERT HOFFMEISTER, MICHAEL KENNEDY,
            KATRIN KLAIBER, KIMBERLY LASHBROOK,
            WILL MCCOY, MARC RIENZO, JERRY SELLS,
            KEN SJOGREN, DEAN YURKE, TODD VAZIRI,
            SUSAN WEEKS, R.D. WEGENER, ERIK WINQUIST,
                  JEFF WOZNIAK, THOMAS ZILS
VFX Production Managers............... LORI ARNOLD
                                     BILL TLUSTY
Hard-Surface Modeling Supervisor..... BRUCE HOLCOMB
Visual Effects Editor .... SCOTT BALCEREK
On-Set Data & Mo Cap Supervisor..... SETH ROSENTHAL
Digital Modelers .... PAMELA J. CHOY,
            FRANK GRAVATT, ALYSON MARKELL,
                  OMZ VELASCO, LI-HSIEN WEI
Viewpaint Artists............... SCOTT BONNENFANT,
            BRIDGET GOODMAN, TONY SOMMERS,
                               DONNA TENNIS
Visual Effects Coordinators......... ANTHONY BUTLER
                                     MEI-MING CASINO
                                     SUSAN GREENHOW

Motion Capture Lead Engineer ...... MICHAEL SANDERS
Motion Capture Technicians............. ALEX FRAZAO
                       DOUG WRIGHT
3D Matchmove Artists .... COLIN BENOIT,
        DUNCAN BLACKMAN, LYDIA CHOY,
        SELWYN EDDY III, LUKE LONGIN,
        DAVID MANOS MORRIS, JAMES SOUKUP,
        TALMAGE WATSON, LAI LAM YIP
Visual Effects Director
   of Photography .... MARTIN ROSENBERG
Model Makers ...... CAROL BAUMAN, NICOLAS BOGLE,
        JON GUIDINGER, NELSON HALL,
        VICTORIA LEWIS, RANDY OTTENBERG,
        ALAN PETERSON, LORNE PETERSON,
        MICHAEL STEFFE, EBEN STROMQUIST,
        DANIEL WAGNER
Practical Effects Supervisor.............. GEOFF HERON
Practical Effects Foreman .... JASON BRACKETT
Stage Support .... RICHARD DEMOLSKI, WILLIAM BARR,
        ROD JANUSCH, FRANK STRZALKOWSKI
Assistant Camera Operator .... BOB HILL
Digital Matte Artists .... JOSHUA ONG
        BRETT NORTHCUTT
Lead Conceptual Designer .... ALEXANDER JAEGER
Storyboard/Concept Design .. BRICE COX, JR., GUS DIZON,
        ERICH IPPEN, ROBERT MACKENZIE,
        AARON MCBRIDE, PHILIP METSCHAN
Lead Digital Paint and Roto Artist .... KATHARINE BAIRD
Digital Paint and Roto Artists .... LANCE BAETKEY,
        CHRIS BAYZ, HUGH BENGS,
        MICHAELA CALANCHINI, DAWN GATES,
        CAM GRIFFIN, JIRI JACKNOWITZ,
        DREW KLAUSNER, JENNIFER MACKENZIE,
        JAKE MAYMUDES, REGAN MCGEE,
        MICHELLE MOTTA, LESLIE SAFLEY,
        SAM STEWART, ALAN TRAVIS, ERIN WEST
Additional Visual Effects Editors NICOLAS ANASTASSIOU
        LORELEI DAVID
        GREG HYMAN
Visual Effects Production Assistants........ KATIE LYNCH
        STEPHEN RIERA
        JESSICA TEACH
Motion Capture Coordinator .... AUDRA KOKLYS
Scanning / Film Recording Operators... ANDREA BIKLIAN
        GEORGE GAMBETTA
        TODD MITCHELL
Software Research & Development .... RYAN KAUTZMAN,
        ANDRE MAZZONE, ZORAN KACIK-ALESIC,
        FLORIAN KAINZ
CG Resource Assistant .... TRINA ESPINOSA
Technical Support .... RALEIGH MANN
Multi-Screen FX Supervisor............. MARK CASEY
Multi-Screen Inferno Artists .... KELA CABRALES
        ORIN GREEN
        CATHERINE TATE
Multi-Screen Production Manager .... DIANE CALIVA
ILM Senior Staff .... CHRISSIE ENGLAND,
        MARK S. MILLER, JIM MORRIS,
        CLIFF PLUMER

In Memory of ERIK GRIEVE

Supervising ADR Editor .. GWENDOLYN YATES WHITTLE
Sound Effects Editors .... KYRSTEN MATE
        DAVID C. HUGHES
        PAUL HSU
Dialogue Editors .... EWA SZTOMPKE-OATFIELD
        RICHARD QUINN
Supervising Assistant Editor............ ANDRE FENLEY
Sound Design Assistant Editor .... DEE SELBY
Dialogue Assistant Editor........... STUART MCCOWEN
ADR Assistant Editor .... JESSICA BELLFORT RANKIN
Re-Recordist .... BRIAN MAGERKURTH
Foley Supervisor .... PAUL URMSON
Foley Editors .... FRANK KERN
        STEVEN VISSCHER
Foley Engineer .... GEORGE A. LARA
Foley Artist..................... MARKO COSTANZO
Effects Assistant.................... LARRY WINELAND
Foley Recording by .... C5, INC.
ADR Mixer........................ DEAN DRABIN
ADR Voice Casting .... BARBARA HARRIS
Executive in Charge of Music
   for Universal Pictures.............. KATHY NELSON
Supervising Music Editor .... ELLEN SEGAL, M.P.S.E.
Additional Music Editor.......... SHIE ROZOW, M.P.S.E.
Score Produced by .... DANNY ELFMAN
Lead Orchestrator.................... STEVE BARTEK
Additional Orchestrations .... EDGARDO SIMONE,
        DAVID SLONAKER, BRUCE FOWLER,
        MARK MCKENZIE, JEFF ATMAJIAN,
        PETE ANTHONY, ROBERT ELHAI
Orchestra Conducted by............... PETE ANTHONY
Score Coordinator .... MARC MANN
Orchestra Contractor.............. DEBBIE DATZ-PYLE
Music Preparation .... JULIAN BRATOLYUBOV
        RON VERMILLION
Score Recorded by............... ROBERT FERNANDEZ
Score Recorded at .. THE FOX NEWMAN SCORING STAGE
Scoring Recordists .... JOHN RODD, NOAH SNYDER,
        GREG DENNEN, RYAN ROBINSON
Score Mixed by .... DENNIS SANDS
Music Mixed at .... EASTWOOD SCORING STAGE
Score Programming...... RANDY KERBER, JUDD MILLER,
        BUCK SANDERS, CLAY DUNCAN,
        ERNIE LEE
Drum Master .... MIKE FISHER

Special Animatronic/Puppet
   Effects by .... K.N.B. EFX GROUP, INC.
Supervisors..................... ROBERT KURTZMAN
        GREG NICOTERO
        HOWARD BERGER
Character Design Maquettes............ RIJN & REISMAN
Opening Sequence & End Title Design .... YU+CO
Visual Designer .... GARSON YU
Inferno Artist .... CONNY FAUSER
Executive Producer.................... JENNIFER FONG
VFX Producer .... PETRA HOLTORF
Opticals by.......... HOWARD ANDERSON COMPANY
Negative Cutter....................... GARY BURRITT
Color Timer........................ ROBERT KAISER

SOUNDTRACK ON DECCA / UMG SOUNDTRACKS

"Mother"
Written by Mychael Danna

"Young Scientists
Written by Danny Elfman & Kenny Burgomaster

"Hulk Escapes"
Written by Danny Elfman, Don Harper & Trevor Morris

Featured Vocals by Natacha Atlas

"Song For Classical Guitar"
Written by Marc Ferrari & Don Great
Performed by Don Great
Courtesy Marc Ferrari & Tinseltown Music

The Producers Wish to Thank

California Department of Forestry & Fire Protection,
Mountain Home Demonstration State Forest
U.S. Department of the Interior, Bureau of Land
Management, Barstow Field Office
Honorable Mayor Willie Brown
City and County of San Francisco
San Francisco Film Commission
Utah Film Commission
Dell Computer Corporation
Corning, Inc.
Fisher Scientific International, Inc.
VWR International, Inc.
Panasonic Consumer Electronics Company
Pepsi-Cola
Labconco Corporation
Coherent Laser Division
Carl Zeiss, Inc.
Northrop Grumman Systems Corporation,
Electronic Systems
Hardigg® Cases - A Division of Hardigg Industries, Inc.
Central Research Laboratories
InnerSpace/Datel™
Cell Press

Albert Einstein ™ HUJ, Represented by The Roger Richman
Agency, Inc. www.therichmanagency.com

American National Red Cross logo used with permission.

Artwork by Arnold Mesches used with permission.

Cameras supplied by Otto Nemenz.

Camera dollies provided by J.L. Fisher.

Camera cranes & dollies by Chapman / Leonard Studio
Equipment, Inc.

Corbis photos used with permission.

Dr. Richard Feynman image/photograph courtesy of the
Archives, California Institute of Technology and The Estate
of Dr. Richard Feynman.

Footage supplied by TECHTV, Inc.

Generator Bank, Arizona Powerhouse, Hoover Dam © 1990
John Sexton. All rights reserved.

Golden Gate National Parks posters courtesy of Graphic
Artist Michael Schwab and The Golden Gate National Parks
Association.

Photography by Felice Frankel used by permission.

"Pinon - Grand Canyon 1924-26" by Gustave Baumann used
by permission of The Museum of New Mexico, Museum of
Fine Arts.

"Tafel VII" and "Tafel VIII"© 2002 used by permission of the
Ralph M. Parsons Fund and Museum Associates/LACMA.

Telly Savalas under license by CMG Worldwide,
www.cmgww.com.

"West From Big 'C', Late Afternoon" from original negative
by Ansel Adams, UCR/California Museum of Photography,
Sweeney/Rubin Ansel Adams FIAT LUX Collection, University of California at Riverside.

Steel Blossom Fence by Mark Bulwinkle

AMERICAN HUMANE ASSOCIATION MONITORED THE
ANIMAL ACTION. NO ANIMAL WAS HARMED. SCENES
APPEARING TO PLACE ANIMALS IN JEOPARDY WERE
SIMULATED.

FILMED WITH PANAVISION CAMERAS AND LENSES
Color by TECHNICOLOR   KODAK Motion Picture Film

ACKNOWLEDGMENTS

Many people helped with the making of this book. For their invaluable assistance, Newmarket Press would like to thank Melissa Amador, Avi Arad, Pam Blum, Colin Brady, Cindy Chang, Megan Corbet, Deborah Daly, Rodolfo Damaggio, Eddie Egan, Bette Einbinder, Larry Franco, Elizabeth Gelfand, Paul Giacoppo, Rick Heinrichs, Gale Anne Hurd, Steve Kenneally, Ang Lee, David Lee, Tiffany Leitner, Jules Mann, Dennis Muren, David O'Connor, Miles Perkins, Lori Petrini, Jeff Sakson, James Schamus, Angie Sharma, Linda Sunshine, Wilson Tang, and Cheryl Tkach.

ERIC BANA   JENNIFER CONNELLY   NICK NOLTE

AN ANG LEE FILM

HULK

UNIVERSAL PICTURES PRESENTS IN ASSOCIATION WITH MARVEL ENTERPRISES A VALHALLA MOTION PICTURES/GOOD MACHINE PRODUCTION "THE HULK" ERIC BANA JENNIFER CONNELLY SAM ELLIOTT JOSH LUCAS AND NICK NOLTE MUSIC BY DANNY ELFMAN COSTUME DESIGNER MARIT ALLEN EDITOR TIM SQUYRES ACE PRODUCTION DESIGNER RICK HEINRICHS DIRECTOR OF PHOTOGRAPHY FREDERICK ELMES ASC EXECUTIVE PRODUCERS STAN LEE KEVIN FEIGE PRODUCED BY GALE ANNE HURD AVI ARAD JAMES SCHAMUS LARRY FRANCO SPECIAL VISUAL EFFECTS AND ANIMATION BY INDUSTRIAL LIGHT & MAGIC STORY BY JAMES SCHAMUS SCREENPLAY BY JOHN TURMAN AND MICHAEL FRANCE AND JAMES SCHAMUS DIRECTED BY ANG LEE

MARVEL | PG-13 PARENTS STRONGLY CAUTIONED | www.thehulk.com | SOUNDTRACK ON DECCA/UMG SOUNDTRACKS | A UNIVERSAL PICTURE UNIVERSAL
Some Material May Be Inappropriate for Children Under 13
SCI-FI ACTION VIOLENCE, SOME DISTURBING IMAGES AND BRIEF PARTIAL NUDITY
® For rating reasons, go to www.filmratings.com
© 2003 UNIVERSAL STUDIOS
THE HULK AND RELATED COMIC BOOK CHARACTERS ™ & © 2002 MARVEL CHARACTERS, INC.

"SET ME FREE" FROM THE HULK PERFORMED BY SCOTT WEILAND, SLASH, DUFF McKAGAN, MATT SORUM AND DAVE KUSHNER